PEMBROKE CHRONICLES

Karen Cross Proctor

THE History PRESS

Published by The History Press
Charleston, SC
www.historypress.net

First published 2015

Manufactured in the United States

ISBN 978.1.62619.974.3

Library of Congress Control Number: 2015945695

CONTENTS

Contents

Contents

ACKNOWLEDGEMENTS

I would like to thank my husband, John Proctor, for his patience and for sharing his photographic skills in the creation of this book. Thank you to Ed Ledbetter, Mary Ford, Janice Ford and the Pembroke Historical Society for providing many of the images for this book. Finally, thank you to the *Pembroke Mariner* and the *Pembroke Express*, two local newspapers, for giving me the opportunity, over twenty years, to research and write these articles and share them with the residents of the town of Pembroke, Massachusetts, a place with a rich history that we all love so much.

INTRODUCTION

The geographic location of the town of Pembroke, Massachusetts, so close to the cradles of American history—Plymouth and Boston—just naturally seems to indicate that Pembroke would have a rich and illustrious history of its own. From the earliest times when local Native Americans fished in its ponds and hunted in its forests, the area they called Namassakeesett teemed with life-giving food and raw materials that fostered the growth of its native and, later, its European populations.

The Europeans first arrived here in the 1640s as part of a natural expansion of Plimoth Plantation and its environs. They, too, found the abundance of herring and the bounty of natural materials conducive to meeting the needs of their burgeoning population. There were trees for wood and bog iron to create the implements needed to build their homes, not to mention the water power afforded by the North River, Herring and Pudding Brooks and other tributaries to run their mills.

To look at the town on a map today, one would not suspect it had been a cradle of shipbuilding, but in the seventeenth, eighteenth and nineteenth centuries, the North River was home to at least five shipyards on its Pembroke shores, all producing seaworthy vessels. They included Seabury Point, Job's Landing, Turner's Yard, Macy's Yard and, perhaps the best known of all of them, the Brick Kiln Yard.

But what truly makes Pembroke unique are its citizens. The town has been the home of industrious Native Americans, brave Patriots, people of great faith and ordinary citizens bent on creating for themselves and their families a comfortable and prosperous place in which to dwell. Either by birth or by choice, Pembroke is blessed with a citizenry that has made and continues to make a difference in the town, in the commonwealth and in the nation.

Part I

NATIVE AMERICANS

Pembroke's Royal Family

If you are at all familiar with the history of the town of Pembroke, you are aware of the first human inhabitants of our town, the Native Americans. Drawn here partly because of the abundance of herring and other fish in our numerous ponds and waterways, these native people walked, hunted and lived on our lands before the first Europeans made their presence known.

The Massachusetts Native American tribal land extended along the eastern coast of our state and was bounded to the south by the land of the Wampanoags, whose chief, Massasoit, made a treaty with the Pilgrims. The chief of the Massachusetts at that time was Chicataubut, and this tribe numbered about three thousand. A smallpox epidemic around 1631–33 decimated the tribe, killing the chief and reducing the number of his followers to about three hundred. Chicataubut's son Josiah Wampatuck became the new chief.

While the chief's home was at Neponset, the tribe seems to have spent much of its time here in what would become Pembroke, and after the death of his father, in about 1647, Wampatuck moved the tribe here permanently. The tribe members settled on a large tract of land around the Pembroke Ponds that is still known to local historians today as the "Indian Fields."

Josiah Wampatuck married Westamoo, the widow of Alexander, who was the son of Massasoit. She was known as the "Squaw Sachem of

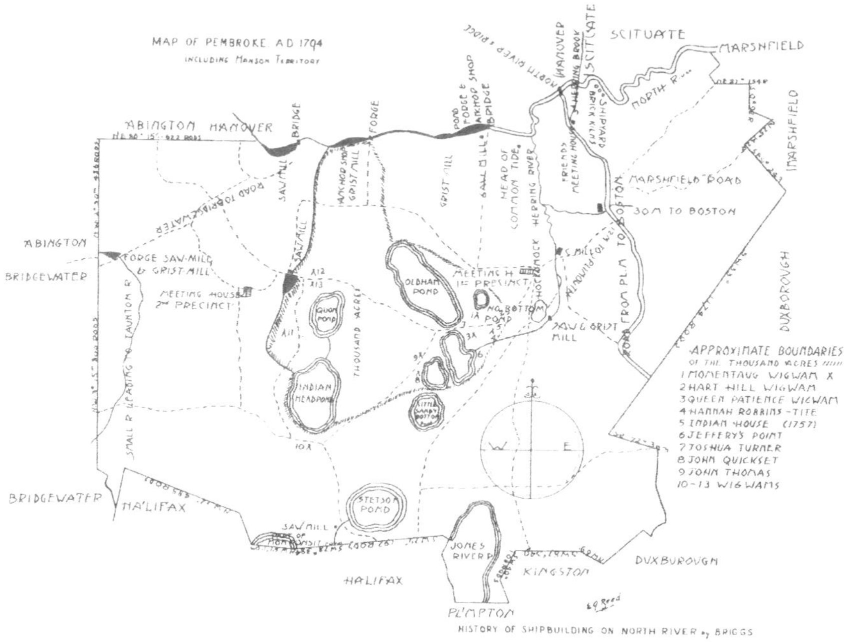

Early map of Pembroke showing the approximate location of the Queen Patience home. *Map drawn by Everett Reed.*

Pocasset." Josiah Wampatuck, who made his home on Furnace Pond, was killed by the Mohawk Indians near Fonda, New York, in 1669. Squamok, brother of Josiah and called Daniel by the English, acted as regent during the time that Josiah and Westamoo's son Charles Josiah Wampatuck was a minor.

Charles Josiah Wampatuck died before 1693 and was succeeded by Abigail Wampatuck Momontaug, the sister of Charles Josiah. She was married to Jeremiah Momontaug. Jeremiah died about 1713, and Abigail died about 1717.

Queen Patience, next in line to be head of the tribe, was the daughter of Abigail and Jeremiah and was married twice—first to Tobias Combs and second to Joseph Peter. Next came Patience's daughter Abigail, then Abigail's son Caleb Brand, then his son Caleb Brand, then James Brand, then son James Brand and Josiah Brand.

The late Russell Gardner of Hanson, a descendant of Pembroke's early Native Americans, dedicated much of his life to collecting the true facts and

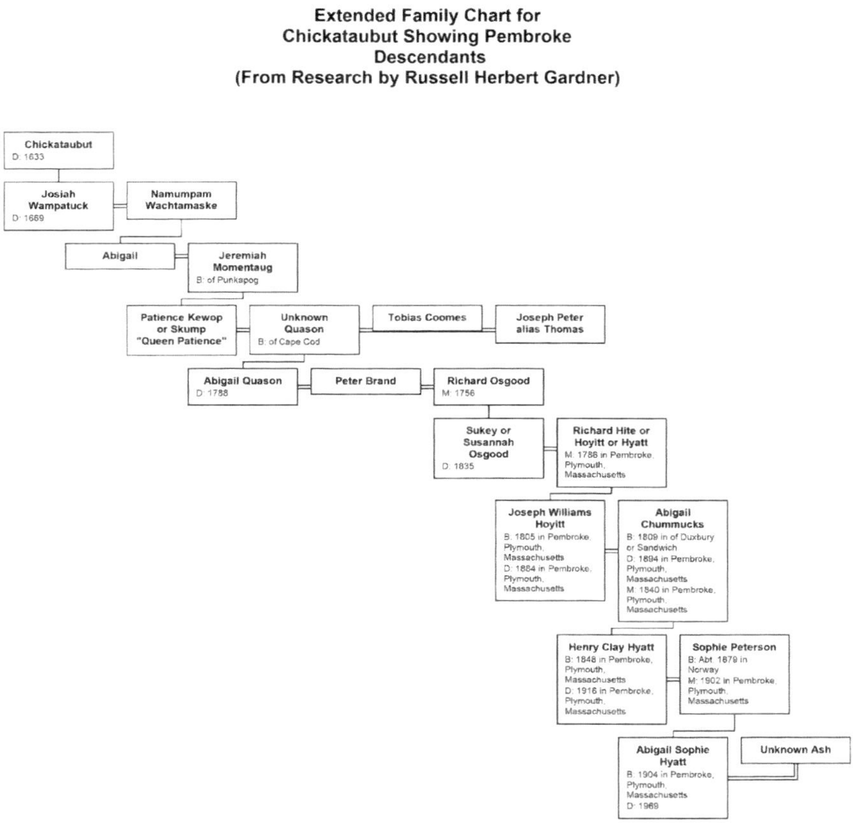

Descendant chart of Pembroke's Native American royal family. *Based on research by Russell Gardner.*

figures pertaining to the legends, folklore and lineage of his ancestors. Based on his research, he put together this lineage of the Massachusetts Native American "Royal Family." These names are found throughout the records of the colony of Massachusetts and the town of Pembroke.

LONG LIVE THE QUEEN!

As most people in Pembroke have come to understand, the Native Americans, so abundant in this area in the years leading up to the twentieth century, have left an indelible mark on our town. Indian Rock,

Early twentieth-century view of the ancestral home of Queen Patience. *From the collection of Ed Leadbetter.*

for example, was named because it was an obvious landmark and meeting place for members of local native groups to gather for trade.

But if you ask most people in Pembroke about Queens Brook, they will direct you to a pleasant road off Center Street. Not everyone is aware of the historic significance of the name. The area was named for a woman of royal Native American ancestry known to those of her time as Queen Patience, or Sunny Eye. The small brook that runs through the area is called Queen's Brook because of its proximity to the home of the last queen of Mattakeesett. Although venerated by all who knew her and heir to thousands of acres of land in the Pembroke-Hanson area, when she died in 1788, she did not actually own as much as a foot of land.

Queen Patience was the great-granddaughter of Chickataubut, the chief sachem (leader) of the Massachusetts Indians at the time when Boston was settled by the English. Although it is said that she married several times, records indicate two marriages. The first marriage was to Tobias Combs and the second to Joseph Thomas. She lived on a point of land that juts out into Furnace Pond. When the traditional Indian wigwam went out of fashion, she conformed to more commonplace ways of living, namely a small cabin, and drew her allotted quota of one hundred herring from the ponds like any other female householder.

Queen Patience float in the 1912 Pembroke bicentennial parade. *Pembroke Historical Society.*

Over the years, Queen Patience sold off much land belonging to the Indians as many of her ancestors had done before her. The town eventually appointed a guardian for the land to keep the remaining acres from becoming depleted.

The queen became the center of many legends. One legend centers on a great pestilence and famine that beset her tribe. Those members of the tribe who had not died gathered at the home of their queen to tell her that they were leaving this place of death and going to seek a new home. Queen Patience told them that she could not leave this place and that she "must die by the graves of my fathers." The rest of the tribe, fearing that she, too, would soon die, left gifts of corn and venison at her door as they fled from the sickness so that she might have food when she was no longer able to hunt or fish.

Queen Patience lived to an advanced age. It is said that she retained her dignity and lofty carriage to the end, refusing aid from the white settlers. Her funeral was attended by the minister of the First Church, as well as many of her neighbors, and she was spoken of highly by all who knew her.

KING PHILIP

A number of years ago, the Pembroke Historical Society was given a most unusual artifact: a human skull. The story that went along with it was even more unusual. It was given to a local man, a descendant of the Native American tribe that once populated our area, with the suggestion that this was the skull of King Philip, namesake of one of the most bloody Indian wars ever fought in southern New England.

King Philip (also known as Metacom or Metacomet) was one of the most interesting of all the New England Indians. He was the great sachem of the Wampanoag Federation from 1662 until he was ambushed and shot on August 12, 1676. He was born about 1640, the younger son of Massasoit, and succeeded to his post of leadership after the death of his older brother, Alexander. This position carried with it great power and influence even though he was only twenty-two years old.

Philip's troubles with the Europeans began almost immediately, for when the English at Plymouth heard of the large gathering of Indians who had come to pay him honor, they assumed he was uniting the New England tribes to war against the English. Philip was summoned to Plymouth to answer questions regarding his intentions. Accompanied by his uncle Akkompoin, the two Wampanoag leaders signed a new treaty with the English.

Upon their return home, younger men of the tribe came to Philip and told him that they wanted to begin hostilities with the Europeans. Philip, following along with his deceased brother's ideas, believed that caution was in order regarding the start of war, even though accepting the authority of the English meant vast changes in the Indians' religion and laws. He tried for some years to keep peace and meet the demands of the European settlers, but the Europeans continued to increase in number and to take over more and more of the Indian lands. The majority of his warriors felt that they should rise in revolt, even if it might mean annihilation if they were unsuccessful. The English began to suspect that Philip was plotting against them secretly and forced the Wampanoags to surrender some of their arms in 1671. Philip was able to gain the cooperation of Canonchet, great sachem of the Narragansett Indians, who had traditionally been hereditary enemies of the Wampanoags. The two young leaders (Canonchet was about the same age as Philip) began planning their course of action.

In 1675, an Indian who was acting as an informer to the colonists was murdered, and three Wampanoags were hanged for the crime. This act triggered the bloody war that eventually involved the Nipmucs as well as the Wampanoags and the Narragansetts. It spread up and down the

Connecticut River Valley in Massachusetts, as well as to the Plymouth and Rhode Island colonies. King Philip was hunted down and killed in a swamp in Rhode Island on August 12, 1676. His death ended the war in southern New England. King Philip's head was impaled on a pole and displayed in Plymouth for more than twenty years.

In the 1720s, Cotton Mather wrote that King Philip's skull was still on the courthouse roof and that he had climbed the pole on which it was impaled to remove the jawbone. It seems that some people in Plymouth were complaining that they could hear Philip's voice at night crying or wailing from the skull. Others claimed that over the years birds had pecked a hole in the back of the skull and nested in it.

No one seemed exactly sure what became of the skull. It was believed that it had not been given a "proper burial" because part of Philip's punishment (as if beheading and quartering his body wasn't enough) was that he should never be given a final resting place.

The skull that was given to the Pembroke Historical Society had been in the possession of a private family from the Silver Lake area for about one hundred years. The family claimed that it was indeed the skull of King Philip, although specific details were sketchy and shrouded in family legend. The skull did, however, have an irregular hole punched in the back and was missing the jawbone. Also, the geographical location (in Plymouth County) lent some credence to the family claims.

Over the years, the historical society and its representatives tried to return the skull to members of the local Native American community, but for reasons that are unclear, the skull remained in Pembroke.

In 1992, a professional portrait artist from Vermont contacted me with questions about the skull. He had seen an article written by the skull's donor in an archaeological publication. For him, it looked like the end of a long quest.

Ever since he could remember, he had been interested in early colonial history. He had read about the celebrated Indian chief, and about ten years earlier, he set out to do a portrait of Philip. The king had never been painted in life, as had so many other notable figures of his time, and of course, he lived before the time of photography, so his likeness had always been a mystery.

For the next ten years, this artist searched museums and other historical institutions for King Philip's skull, refusing to believe that it no longer existed. He hoped to make a plastic-like casting of the skull, which could then be fashioned with clay into a fairly accurate likeness of this famous Native American. While it is believed that King Philip's wife and son were either executed or sent to the West Indies, this artist had uncovered several nineteenth-century photos of descendants of Philip and had also met and photographed two twentieth-century descendants, albeit obviously from different branches of Philip's family tree. The artist was willing, with the historical society's permission, to pay to have the skull analyzed by Dr. William Bass, director of forensic anthropology at the University of Tennessee. So on July 22, 1992, I packed up "Phil," as he had become known to my family, and sent him off to Tennessee (but not without some rather quizzical looks from the employees of the mail store where I brought him for packaging!).

The results were interesting. The skull was indeed that of an American Indian man. However, skull development indicated that he was between the ages of seventeen and twenty-one when he died. King Philip was believed to have been between the ages of thirty and forty when he died. The skull had been buried (a light tan dirt remained in many of the crevices). The dark brown color of the skull indicated burial in a wooden coffin. Also, if the skull had been exposed to the elements "for a generation," then it would be sun-bleached and show weathering, which this skull did not. These findings indicated to Dr. Bass that this was not the skull of King Philip. I never heard from the portrait artist again.

A short time later, it was brought to the attention of the historical society that through the Massachusetts Historical Commission and with the blessing of the Massachusetts Archaeological Society, Native American remains could be returned to the Native American authorities for proper repatriation. Connie Crosby, a Pembroke resident who was an archaeologist with the Massachusetts Historical Commission, took possession of "King Philip." He was finally returned to his people.

I can't help but think that somewhere the soul of a young local Native American is finally at peace. It is important to note that anyone finding Native American remains should work with any of the above-named authorities to return them to the Native American community for proper burial. We would want no less for any of our ancestors.

Part II

PEMBROKE'S FAMILIES

The Browns, a Family of Quakers

Over the last several years, I've done a lot of research preparing to write these columns. Sometimes, much to my disappointment, I discovered that some local legends did not stand up to careful scrutiny. Other times, I've been delighted to discover that long-held traditions are basically true—with some slight modifications over the years.

For years, there was a locally held belief among historians that a tiny, almost unknown family cemetery, located off High Street, contained the remains of a Brown family with close ties to the founders of the Ivy League college Brown University in Providence, Rhode Island. The indications are there—one stone contains the name Moses Brown, which was also the name of one of Brown University's founders. There is also a Pembroke Hall, which is part of Brown University.

So, with too much time on my hands, I decided to tackle this thorny, if not particularly pressing, historical conundrum. It was time consuming although not particularly difficult to put together the details, which I relay here.

Brown University was actually founded in 1764 by the Baptist Church and called Rhode Island College. The wealth of Rhode Island centered on the merchants of Newport, and among these families was the family of James Brown and his four sons—Nicholas, Joseph, John and Moses—all eminent merchants in their own right. They were descendants of immigrant ancestor Chad Brown, who became pastor of the First Baptist Church in Providence in 1642.

Moses Brown family cemetery. *Photo by John Proctor.*

For reasons including money and property ownership, as well as other considerations, in 1804, the school changed its name to Brown University, named for James's son Nicholas Brown, "a devout man, although he never joined any church: he believed in the distinct doctrines of the Baptists and came from an old Rhode Island family." Part of the university was built on land sold to it in 1770 by John and Moses Brown. Pembroke Hall, built in 1897, took its name from the college at England's Cambridge University, founded by the countess of Pembroke and attended by Roger Williams, founder of the colony of Rhode Island.

The Moses Brown buried in Pembroke came from the same Brown family, descended from Chad Brown. The Pembroke Browns were Quakers. Apparently, part of the family converted to Quakerism during our Moses's great-grandfather's generation. Our Moses was born in 1835 and died in 1861. His parents were Samuel and Marie (Hussey?) Brown. Samuel's parents were Smith and Lydia (Gould) Brown. Smith's parents were Elisha and Martha (Smith) Brown. This is where the connection comes in to the Brown University family. It seems that Elisha (our Moses's great-grandfather) was the brother of James Brown, whose sons were the "four brothers," Nicholas, Joseph, John and Moses. As mentioned earlier, Brown University was actually named after the brother Nicholas.

So, there you have it. The namesake of Brown University was the great-great-uncle of our Moses. OK, it's very remote, but the connection is there, thus proving that some legends do pan out under careful scrutiny and confirming my faith in some historical legends.

This brings us to the identities of the six inhabitants of the Brown family cemetery, all members of the Samuel and Maria Brown family. Samuel Brown was born in Providence in 1787, the child of Smith and Lydia Brown. He married Maria (Hussey) in Nantucket, where Maria was born, and settled in Pembroke, where four of their eight children were born. Four of their children—Ann, Sarah Joy, Lydia G. and Joseph G.—also appear as having been born in Pembroke and Nantucket, which may have been a mistake and occurred when the family moved to Pembroke and registered with the Quaker meeting here.

Not all of their children are buried here in the family plot with them; Ann, George, Joseph, Lydia Brown Randall and William Austin Brown are elsewhere. Moses Brown, Elizabeth Brown Wood and Sarah Joy Brown are buried here with their parents.

Samuel, the patriarch, died in Pembroke in 1868 of "old age." He was eighty-one years old. His wife, Maria, also died in Pembroke in 1868 of

The Moses Brown home on High Street. *Pembroke Historical Society.*

"congestion of lungs." She was seventy-five years old. Their son Moses died here in 1861 of "inflammation of the bowels." Unfortunately, he apparently did not get the longevity gene from his parents, as he was only twenty-six years old when he died. He was not married. Sarah Joy Brown died in 1891 of cancer. She, too, was unmarried and lived to be seventy years of age. Elizabeth B. Wood was the wife of Jabel Wood. She died in 1868 in Lynn, Massachusetts, but was buried here in the family plot. She died of "gastric fever" and was forty years old.

The final inhabitant of the Brown Cemetery is Lydia Brown. She was the unmarried sister of Samuel. Born in 1798, she died in 1883, making her eighty-five years of age.

Looking at federal census records for the family in Pembroke, it appears that the large farmhouse was always full of people. They always had extended family, as well as those less fortunate, living with them. For example, in 1860, they had an Amy Otis, "spinster," under their roof. They also appear to have been well educated by some standards, as Moses and Sarah listed themselves as teachers in 1860. Elizabeth called herself a "dressmaker" in the same census.

Although devout Quakers, instead of being interred in the cemetery next to the Friends Meetinghouse, Samuel, a farmer, decided to bury his family in a small private plot in a corner of the Brown family farm, which was located on High Street.

THE MAGOUN FAMILY

John Magoun came from Scotland to Massachusetts in about 1655. He first settled in Hingham and then came to the Pembroke area in about 1665. John and his wife, Rebecka, were among the earliest settlers of the area known as the "Two Mile," which encompassed Water Street and was formerly part of Scituate. He purchased a tract of land, it is believed, from Robert and Lucy Barker and, in 1666, built a home, which is still standing on Water Street. This home is considered one of the oldest buildings in Pembroke today.

The house was built with two stories in the front, sloping down to one story (a lean-to) in the rear. It consisted of two rooms with a hall between and had a large central chimney The land behind the house extended down to the North River, which later became a cradle of New England wooden shipbuilding and would feature prominently in the lives of later Magouns who were shipbuilders. The earliest generations of Magouns were farmers.

Magoun family cemetery. *Photo by John Proctor.*

At his death in 1708, John Magoun left the property to his son, the second John Magoun. The property was expanded and improved by John Magoun and Luther Magoun, descendants of the first John.

A grandson of the first John Magoun, Recompense Magoun, built a gambrel-style home in East Pembroke.

A later generation of Magouns—Elias and his wife, Esther (Sampson) Magoun—inherited the Water Street ancestral home. Being devout Methodists, they always kept the upstairs left chamber for a meeting of fellow Methodists who came from as far away as Duxbury. This room became known as the "Prophet's Chamber." The old homestead passed out of the Magoun family in 1893. Since then, there have been many owners and many changes to the original structure.

Water Street was also the site of the homes of Asaph and Paul Magoun. The Paul Magoun Cemetery on Water Street is one of five small family plots in the former Two Mile area. The names of Turner and Magoun lead the list of those interred there.

Other Magoun family members built homes in the area of Brick Kiln Lane and Washington Street. The homes of Thatcher Magoun and Aaron Magoun were located in this area.

The small, once private cemetery on the corner of Water Street and Route 139 consisting of about fifty or so stones is historically known as the

The Magoun house as it appears today. *Photo by John Proctor.*

Luther Magoun Cemetery. Interred therein are members of the Magoun (also spelled Magoon and Magume) and several related families. One of the earliest stones is that of Hannah (Macfarland) Magoun, wife of Elias Magoun, who died on October 26, 1707, at the age of twenty-seven. This Elias was another son of John and Rebecka Magoun.

Anyone who has children who play sports in Pembroke is probably familiar with the Magoun Field located near the intersection of Washington Street (Route 53) and Schooset Street (Route 139) named for this longtime Pembroke family.

THE PARRIS FAMILY

The roots of the town of Pembroke extend back to a hearty band of colonists who were weary of the long journey to Sunday church services in Duxbury. They began to meet in an apple orchard belonging to Joseph Rogers that was located off Mountain Avenue. This spot became known as Sabbaday Orchard. The establishment of a new church based on the Sabbaday Orchard band of settlers resulted in the establishment of the town of Pembroke in 1712.

One of Joseph Rogers's daughters, Abigail, had married Thomas Parris, a man with "book learning" and, according to Pembroke historian Harry Litchfield, a willing speaker. One of Parris's closest friends was Edward Thompson, a crusading pastor from Marshfield. Some of Thompson's fiery spirit had rubbed off on Parris, and he became a leader of the Sabbaday Orchard group. By 1708, Parris's congregation had moved to a meetinghouse built on the spot where the First Church stands today. In 1712, an ordained minister, the Reverend Daniel Lewis, was settled at the Pembroke meetinghouse, and the town had what it needed to become established.

Thomas Parris was the son of John Parris of London, England. Thomas had come first to Long Island in 1683; married his first wife, Mary; and moved to Boston, where Mary died, leaving Thomas with two daughters to raise alone. In 1697, Thomas moved to that part of Duxbury that became Pembroke, where he met and married his second wife, Abigail, the aforementioned daughter of Joseph Rogers and Abigail Barker. Their homestead was located behind the present site of Pembroke Town Hall. Records indicate that Joseph and Abigail were the parents of at least seven children, and when Abigail died in 1713, it appears that Thomas married Grace Record a year later.

The late local historian Sarah E. Bosworth tells a story that indicates a more unsavory side to Thomas Parris: "I've heard from Grandmother Osborne of the wrongs of the Parrises to the Indians which finally ended by a member of the family getting the seeds of small pox and sowing them among the Indians which finally exterminated them. Most people of that generation believed firmly [that the house was haunted] until it passed from the name."

In January 1716, the Town of Pembroke voted "that scoll be kept half a year annually in ye middle of town by ye meeting house." It is believed that this first schoolhouse was located directly across the street from the meetinghouse on the site of the present Pembroke Historical Society Museum. The first schoolmaster was Thomas Parris. He also served as town clerk.

The Parris family grew and prospered in towns throughout the South Shore. Perhaps the most famous member of the Parris family was Alexander Parris, world-renowned architect. Alexander was born in 1780 in Halifax, Massachusetts. His family moved to Maine when he was a child and then to North Pembroke when Alexander was a teenager. Early in his life, he became an apprentice carpenter and worked at the more practical side of his craft, all the while purchasing and studying books on design. He soon earned a reputation locally for his house designs and attention to detail. By the time he was twenty years old, he had become a talented architect. He soon married Pembroke resident Sylvia Stetson and moved to Portland, Maine.

While in Portland, he built a home for a navy commodore and was given the opportunity to rebuild the forts in Portland Harbor. Unfortunately, the 1807 embargo caused a severe economic slowdown, and Alexander had difficulty finding work. He eventually moved to Boston. During this period, he traveled to the cities of Richmond, Philadelphia and New York.

When the War of 1812 began, Alexander served as a captain in the Army Corps of Engineers. After the war, he returned to Boston and joined a small group of architects who studied under the influence of Charles Bulfinch. Bulfinch was a Boston architect and designer of the Massachusetts State House and the national Capitol in Washington, D.C.

Alexander proved to be one of Bulfinch's most talented students and soon developed his own following. Between 1818 and 1821, he worked on Massachusetts General Hospital. In 1825, he designed Quincy Market as part of a Boston waterfront redevelopment project. He also designed the Charlestown Navy Yard, and he built the Chelsea Navy Hospital and Pilgrim Hall in Plymouth. In 1837, he was called on to design the third (and current) First Church Meetinghouse in Pembroke. During his lifetime, Alexander designed many other notable structures, as well as private residences.

In 1852, while returning from a trip to Washington, D.C., Alexander became gravely ill and died at his home on Washington Street in Pembroke. He and his wife are buried in the Briggs Burial Ground near his home.

THE PEARCE FAMILY

When we think of the first settlers of Pembroke, we tend to think of the Barker family, but another important, lesser-known family who settled in Pembroke in the beginning was the family of Abraham Pearce (also spelled Pierce and a variety of other ways). Abraham arrived in the Pembroke area shortly after the Barkers—in fact, his descendants traced him back to his arrival on the ship *Anne*, which landed at Plymouth in 1623. It is believed that Abraham was one of two passengers listed only as "Capt. Perce's servants."

By 1637, Abraham Pearce was living in what would later become the town of Kingston, but by 1643, he shows up on the rolls of Duxbury (of which Pembroke was a part until 1712). He had been granted land on the banks of the Namassakeset Brook, near where the Barker family garrison

The Pearce family home. *Pembroke Historical Society.*

was located (at the corner of Barker and High Streets). He cleared the land and chose, as the spot for his house, a plot of rising land halfway between the Barker garrison and the hill that would later become the site of the Pembroke Meetinghouse.

Not always acting with the best of behavior, in 1651 he appeared before the grand jury for spending the Sabbath slothfully and negligently and not frequenting public worship, a charge from which he was later excused but warned to mend his ways.

The Pearce family prospered, and more land was granted to them. By the incorporation of the town of Pembroke in 1712, the family owned a large portion of what would become Pembroke center. Abraham died around 1673, and his land was divided among his sons (Abraham, Isaac and James) while his daughters (Rebecca, Mary and Alice) each received twenty shillings.

Abraham Jr. held the land at Highgary (another name for the land that became Center Pembroke) and, early in the history of the town, sold a section of his land as part of the site of the present Center Cemetery.

Colonial records indicate that Abraham Jr. was quite a colorful character. In 1661, he admitted that he had defamed Rebecca Alden and Hester Delaney, and in 1663, he was arraigned before the court for abusive speeches against his father. Despite all this, in 1673, he was appointed executor of his father's estate. Abraham Pearce Jr. was married twice and had three sons and one daughter. He died in 1718.

Abraham III, son of Abraham Jr., was elected several times to be "tithing man." His duties were to inspect all licensed and unlicensed houses where it was suspected that gaming or tippling was being carried out for profit or where "strong drink" was being sold. He was also to inspect "the manners of all disorderly Persons" and report on "all persons whose conduct tends to debauchery, irreligion, prophaneness or atheism." As if those duties didn't keep him busy enough, he was also elected highway surveyor, constable, collector of town and parish taxes and juryman.

The Tubbs Family and Their Meadow

Have you taken a walk through Pembroke's open space triumph, Tubbs Meadow Preserve? It is, without a doubt, one of the town's crowning jewels and well worth visiting at any time of year. While researching the origin of the name Tubbs Meadow, I have discovered some interesting bits and pieces relating to various members of the Tubbs family in the early records of Pembroke.

The family was in the area that would become Pembroke at an early date. In 1710, when land known as Marshfield Upper Common Lands (which would eventually be joined with other parcels to become Pembroke) was divided into lots, the name Tubbs Meadow was already part of the vernacular. The term appears in the descriptions of several of the set-out lots. For example, lot 50 mentions "21 poles to stones at the foot of the hill by side of meadow ground called Tubbs Meadow."

William and Joseph Tubbs were signers of a petition for the inclusion of the Mattakeesett section (which was part of northwest Duxbury) in the incorporation of the new town of Pembroke in 1712. This may be the William Tubbs who is buried in the Center Cemetery. His stone said he died August 15, 1718, at age sixty-three and is considered one of the earliest burials in that cemetery. Deacon Samuel Tubbs appears to have paid Queen Patience for lease of Indian land from 1763 to 1765. Simeon, Daniel and

Ephraim Tubbs from Pembroke served in the French and Indian War in Captain Abel Keen's Company, circa 1756 to 1758.

In a letter written by Mrs. A.K. Tillson to A.J. Bryant sometime between 1884 and 1890, Mrs. Tillson recalled some of the old houses in Pembroke. She wrote:

> *Widow Abigail Bearce was a Tubbs* [born March 1, 1722/3, the daughter of William and Abigail (Bonney) Tubbs; married Thomas Bearce of Halifax in 1743/4]. *She was a widow some 60 years and was called Granny Bearce. She lived in a hut with two small windows of diamond glass set in lead. It stood on the left hand between the Tubbs meadow and Thomas J. Turner's. She had three children, Ichabod, Benjamin and Abigail…I think this house, with only one room and rough in all respects as you can imagine, was not her former home, but was built for her after her children were married. I think in her husband's day, she lived near where Hector Monroe (Monroe Street) now lives.*

Apparently, Mrs. Tillson was asked about the Tubbs Mill because she continued, "I don't seem to remember about the mill…but E.W. Tillson says he knows where it was and could find the place where it stood."

Mrs. Tillson's letter is the only place I can find a mention of the legendary Tubbs Mill said to be located on the Tubbs Meadow Brook.

Finally, I came across two letters relating to the misfortunes of at least two members of this elusive family. The story they portrayed with such a lack of compassion reminded me of how the phrase "the good old days" can sometimes ring hollow. You can see the early roots of today's child welfare system beginning to take hold.

The letter was addressed to "The Gent. Overseers of the Poor, Pembroke, Mass" and was postmarked "Northampton, Mass., May 1821." The letter writer was Norris or Harris (old handwriting is sometimes difficult to decipher) Hatch. It began, "By request, I have been supplying the Tubs woman with som artacels. She has a child four weaks old. It come more than two months sooner then she swore it wood. We believe she swore it on the rong man. There has two men run off before there was any stur for fear of being taken and whare they be we no not. There is no prospect at present of gitting aney thing. I hav put out her child. She is eight years old."

The letter went on to say that the eight-year-old child had no clothes except rags that were replaced by the family that took her in. This kind family felt that since she was in good health and they seemed to like her, they

Tubbs Meadow Brook. *Photo by John Proctor.*

would not charge the Town of Pembroke for her new "duds," as they put it. However, if they decided not to keep her, they "must" have ten dollars. Mr. Hatch felt that the family would probably keep the child until she turned eighteen and went on to ask the overseers to allow the child to remain with the family "if that be your mind." He described the child's natural mother as "the poorest carrictur we have in town; the truth is not to be found in her" and that "she was very much afraid of being carried to Pembroke."

This thoughtful person was not planning to do any more for the woman than was absolutely necessary and felt that his efforts were worth about nine dollars. He also felt that she should be returned to Pembroke to make her own way, as she was "as abel as any other woman," and warned that if the woman stayed in his town, she was likely to have more children and become more of a burden to Pembroke. He finished his letter by announcing that he would come to Pembroke in the fall with his account book to receive his payment.

The second letter was by Rodney Starkweather, whose family had taken in the little eight-year-old girl. He promised that he would give the child "a good common education with attention paid to her morals." He "bound himself to take care of the child in sickness and in health until she turns eighteen years of age."

We will probably never know what happened to the woman—did she come back to Pembroke? Did her newborn child survive? Did the eight-year-old girl grow up to be a productive citizen of Northampton? We can only hope.

There is further mention of various Tubbs family members in town records right up until the twentieth century. It is unclear when the family name died out in Pembroke, but it will live on forever in the stream, meadow and now nature preserve bearing the Tubbs name.

Part III

STORIES OF OUR CITIZENS

Gleason Archer, Blueberry Farmer and Lawyer

Often, when Pembroke residents decide to attend law school, Suffolk University in Boston is one of the schools they might investigate. I'm not sure, however, how many realize that this well-known school was actually founded by a former Pembroke resident and blueberry farmer.

Gleason Archer, LLD, was born about 1880 in Plantation #33, Hancock County, Maine, the son of a blacksmith. About 1900, he left rural Maine for law school in Boston. From a modest apartment in Roxbury, he attended law school while earning money washing floors in a "hash house" on Staniford Street and later as a waiter at Floyd's restaurant at South Station.

In 1906, after passing the bar, rather than taking a job at a law firm, he decided to make a career teaching other "poor boys" to become lawyers. From that same Roxbury apartment, he began to teach nine "enthusiastic, but desperately poor" workingmen. Within sixteen years, he was at the helm of a large school specializing in night education and "in giving the poor boy a chance."

In a newspaper article by Francis X. Clement, Archer said, "I have modeled my school on no other school, nor have I studied systems of teaching. Instead, I have devised a plan of my own. Many people have complained about it, but the results speak for themselves. A poor man has the right to study law and become a lawyer if he so desires."

Remnants of blueberry bushes from Gleason Archer's blueberry farm. *Photo by John Proctor.*

There were no rigid entrance exams; a high school education was suggested, but if, after talking to an applicant, Archer deemed him to have the brainpower necessary to pursue a law education, he was allowed into the school.

The school was growing, and its graduates were going on to prominent positions in Massachusetts legal life, but it could not confer degrees. After a lengthy legal battle with then Massachusetts governor Eugene Foss, new governor David Walsh signed the bill on March 10, 1914, and Suffolk Law School was legitimate.

In August 1920, Governor Calvin Coolidge laid the cornerstone for a new building at Temple and Derne Streets.

In 1934, the College of Liberal Arts and Sciences opened at Suffolk University.

Eventually, the founder of this highly esteemed school and author of thirteen law textbooks, as well as several other books, came to Pembroke to run his Archer's Blueberry Nursery at the corner of Old Washington and High Streets.

JOHN GILBERT BONNEY'S DRUM

In the spring of 1999, the Pembroke Historical Society was given a wonderful gift—a ceremonial drum owned by John Gilbert Bonney of Pembroke.

It was given by the Gerraughty family of Hanson as the completion of a last wish of Mrs. Gerraughty's father, John Sabin. Mr. Sabin, an insurance agent and drummer from Abington, had seen the drum in the garage of one of his clients and had asked if he could buy it. The owner had stipulated that he could buy the drum only if he promised that the drum be given to the Pembroke Historical Society after Sabin's death. John Sabin died in 1996.

John Gilbert Bonney was born in Pembroke in 1832 or 1833 (two different records give two different birth years). He was the son of James Bonney and Catherine (Magoun) Bonney. Generations of the Bonney and Magoun families had lived in Pembroke since the town's incorporation. In 1862, John enlisted in the Union army, Company A, Third Massachusetts Infantry, and served as a drummer/musician until he mustered out in 1863. Returning to his native Pembroke, he remained here and probably worked as a housewright until his death in 1891 at the age of fifty-nine. He is buried in the Center Cemetery.

John Gilbert Bonney's drum. *Photo by John Proctor.*

The drummer's job was to beat cadence for his unit while marching and establish communications in the field using many different drum calls for everything from assembling the officers for meetings to sounding retreat. He stood near a high-ranking officer in case he was needed to alert troops to some impending action.

The leather-trimmed drum still had its original rawhide drumheads and gold leaf. It was adorned with an eagle and banners where the names J.G. Bonney and Pembroke were printed. There was no maker's mark, but a label on the inside of the drum read, "18 May 1886."

It was originally believed that the drum was actually used in the war, but a local Civil War expert, having made a careful inspection of the piece, believed that it was, in fact, ceremonial and probably was used for functions of the GAR (Grand Army of the Republic, a fraternal organization for Union Civil War veterans).

The drum is currently on display in a special case that protects it from dust and dirt.

The Mystery That Was Dr. Charles Boucher

About forty years ago, South Shore historian Curt Norris wrote an article about Pembroke's Dr. Charles Boucher—"Old Doc," as he was known around here in the 1920s. I found it fascinating and thought the story was worth retelling.

It seems that Mr. Norris's parents, Boston newspaper people, were sent to Pembroke to do a story on an aged doctor living in Pembroke who was supposed to have a gander who followed him everywhere. Their editor thought it might make a nice Sunday feature.

Apparently, Old Doc took a liking to the family at their first interview, for they eventually spent the entire summer in a tiny camp located behind the doctor's two-hundred-year-old farmhouse here in town that Dr. Boucher shared with Propaganda, the gander; two police dogs, Minnie and Fritz; and assorted chickens and ducks.

Mr. Norris described Old Doc as "tall, ram-rod straight, with a Van Dyke beard and a full head of white hair." His legs were slightly bowed due to years in the cavalry. He possessed "twinkling blue eyes, a crusty sense of humor and a kindly soul."

A few details of his life before Pembroke were known. He told them that he was a native of Paris, where he had earned his medical degree. He came to the United States at the beginning of the twentieth century and opened a dispensary on Harrison Street in Boston. He was first noticed in Pembroke by folks who remembered him as suddenly showing up looking prosperous and distinguished in a big raccoon coat. Soon, local children were bringing their sick pets to see "Uncle Doc."

Mr. Norris remembered that the doctor had some unorthodox medical beliefs, such as the importance of walking barefoot outside so that the electricity in the ground could connect with the electricity in our bodies for a beneficial effect.

But most interesting of all were the late-evening talks sitting around a kerosene lamp listening to Old Doc recounting his younger days in Europe. He told of his studies under the famed Louis Pasteur, of his three years traveling around the world and of living for a year with a fisherman in Hammerfest and later in India, where he was offered one of the wives of an Indian ruler. As fantastic as the stories were, Mr. Norris always reminded himself that the man was fluent in eight languages, so surely anything was possible. But perhaps most remarkable of all were the doctor's accounts of being the consulting physician for the archduke of Serbia and his stories of actress Katherine Schratt, dancing with Princess Stephanie and being present at the first playing of "On the Beautiful Blue Danube."

His stories were wonderful and far removed from his surroundings in the woods of Pembroke in the 1920s. Mr. Norris's parents were newspaper people, however, and rather skeptical. When Dr. Boucher died in 1934 and the family stood around the unmarked grave site along with Boston policemen, city officials, reporters and townspeople from Pembroke, Curt and his parents believed that the true story of Dr. Boucher's life had died with him.

A few years after the doctor's death, acquaintances of the Norris family found themselves being introduced to a countess who had been raised on the grounds of the old Viennese palace. When asked if she had ever heard of Dr. Charles Boucher, she answered, "A man who would be in his eighties now? He always wore a Van Dyke and walked like this?" She demonstrated the walk of a person who had spent much time on a horse. "Yes, I knew such a man when I was a very little girl. He was physician to Archduke Ferdinand." He had apparently also tended to the young countess on occasion.

Proof of the life Dr. Boucher had lived and spoken of so many years before? Not exactly written in concrete but certainly tantalizingly close to corroboration by an eyewitness.

All of this aroused my curiosity, and so with my Nancy Drew hat on, I did a little checking on my own. By checking the doctor's death certificate, I learned that Charles E. Boucher was actually born in Wyoming, Illinois, in 1858, the son of Fred Boucher, who was born in Paris, and Harriett Bent, who was born in California. It is possible that the family had moved back to the father's homeland after the birth of Charles, but he was not born in France. Louis Pasteur lived from 1822 until 1895, so it is possible that Charles had been a student of his. "On the Beautiful Blue Danube" was written by Strauss and performed in 1867, so if Dr. Boucher had been present during its first performance, he would have been about nine years old—again, not out of the realm of possibility. Archduke Franz Ferdinand was born in 1863 and assassinated in 1914, so this timing also makes his claim possible.

So were Dr. Charles Boucher's claims the ramblings of a lonely old man with advanced arteriosclerosis or had he led the incredible life he claimed? To me, the pros outweigh the cons, and the main sticking point—his place of birth—could possibly have been a misunderstanding in the recounting of the story. Over its history, Pembroke has been the home of a number of fascinating people, both native and adopted, and I think Old Doc can be added to this illustrious list.

Edith's Hat

Local historical societies are the repositories for all types of antique artifacts ranging from important documents to heirlooms that families wish to share with the community. Sometimes, these donations come with information about who owned them or what specific role the artifact played within a family. Often, there is very little background information on a piece except the purpose for which it was used. On a very rare occasion, a donation is made of a particular piece that has a special history, well documented and sometimes even very moving.

Local history, after all, is really made up of hundreds of personal human stories woven together for the larger effect. The objects left behind by people, therefore, may be an integral part of that personal history.

One such object, a child's leghorn hat, was donated to the Pembroke Historical Society a short time ago by Mrs. Marie Manson of Boston, who tells its story as follows:

Edith's hat. *Photo by John Proctor.*

Gravestone of Edith Lewis and her family at Sachem Lodge Cemetery. *Photo by John Proctor.*

Edith Lewis was the daughter of George and Sarah Lewis. She was born on October 2, 1868. Her father, George, was an able seaman who held a first mate's license but was unable to make the grade of captain because of color blindness. He went to sea for long periods of time, and for this reason, his wife, Sarah, and Edith, the little girl, made their home with Sarah's parents, Francis and Lydia (Cole) Merritt, at their house on High Street near the Pembroke–West Duxbury line.

In the late 1870s, George shipped out aboard a vessel that remained at sea for two or three years. When the voyage was completed and he returned to the port of New York, George made a special shopping trip for gifts for his family. For his daughter, Edith, he purchased a child's leghorn hat. It was of such exquisite workmanship and beauty that it must have come from a very special city millinery shop.

Unfortunately, when George arrived home, Edith was either in the last stages of valvular disease of the heart, which was listed as her official cause of death, or she had already passed away. Edith, with other members of her family, is buried in the little Pembroke cemetery off High Street (known as the Loring family cemetery or Sachem Lodge Cemetery). Her gravestone gives her death date as November 16, 1880, at age twelve years, one month and fourteen days. Her hat was never worn but has been lovingly cared for by members of her family for over one hundred years.

Elliott Ford

If you lived in town anytime before 1998, you may remember one of Pembroke's favorite citizens, Elliott Ford. He was the town handyman, but for me, he was a local historian who had lived his entire life in our town.

I first met Elliott in 1987, when I became curator of the Pembroke Historical Society. I was told I would probably run into him, as he was custodian of our museum building, as well as many of the other buildings in Pembroke Center. Sure enough, one day as I was sitting in the museum trying to become familiar with our files and books, an elderly man wearing a blue baseball cap and blue jacket came through the front door. I introduced myself; he answered with a wonderfully New England sounding "ahyuh" and, without ever actually mentioning his own name, looked around the room and began pointing out various objects and artifacts that he and his brother Alton had donated over the years.

Elliott Ford. *Photo courtesy of Janice and Mary Ford.*

That was the beginning of a cherished and rich acquaintance (at least on my part) with a man whose head was full of stories about old-time Pembroke residents and events. Over the years, I heard (usually more than once) about the disciplinary measures of beloved Pembroke teacher Lydia Drake from a man who remembered Miss Drake. I heard about the escapades of "the boys" who used to hang out at the Hobomock Inn. He told me about his early years as a volunteer fireman for the town. If I had a question about a particular historic house in Pembroke, he could usually be counted on to provide an anecdote about either the house or the former family who had occupied it. I once had an inquiry about a house in town from its owner. Preliminary checking indicated that the house had belonged to Elliott's grandfather, so I suggested that she contact him for more information. She called me back a few minutes later and, chuckling, told me that she had called Elliott and invited him to dinner so they could talk. He had replied, politely, that he did not "do dinner" but that he did "do cookies," so they were going to make arrangements for an afternoon meeting at which she could serve cookies. I don't know if this meeting ever took place, but if it didn't, more's the pity. One of the things I had always planned to do was interview Elliott in depth on so many of the subjects we had touched on over the years and record his responses on videotape. I will always regret that I never "found the time."

Elliott knew the layout of the Center Cemetery like the back of his hand. If someone came to town looking for an ancestor, Elliott could either lead them directly to the appropriate grave or at least steer them in the right direction.

The people of First Church will miss Elliott. Until the end, he rarely missed a Sunday, and that clock was kept wound by him with unfailing regularity. As a special tribute to Elliott, Dewey Jensen stopped the town clock just before the funeral and started it up again after the events of the day.

The Elliott Ford I remember was a kind and gentle soul who had knowledge of local history and the time to share it with others that comes with age.

HARRY WHEATLAND LITCHFIELD, LOCAL HISTORIAN

When we think of the many personalities whose lives have graced the town of Pembroke, one name stands out above the rest. This gentleman and his family gave much to the town, especially in preserving the history of Pembroke. He was a prolific, energetic and enthusiastic writer and recorder of past events without whose lifetime efforts the history of our town would be sadly lacking. His name was Henry Wheatland Litchfield, known to most as Harry. Among his many achievements, he was the author of *Ancient Landmarks of Pembroke*, which was first printed in 1909 and has been reprinted twice since. The following information about his life was written in a biographical sketch that Harry asked his cousin Anne Henderson of Hanover to write for him.

Harry Litchfield was born on Barker Street in Pembroke on May 23, 1886. He was the son of Edwin P. and Alice Whitman Litchfield. When he was two days old, he said, his father gave him a world atlas as a "primer for the boy." By the time he was three, he had learned the alphabet, taught to him by his grandfather Thomas Turner Whitman. It appears that from this early age the importance of books and education was stressed in the Litchfield home. His parents were honest, hardworking people. His father was foreman at the Arnold Shoe Factory in Pembroke, and his mother sang in the choir of the First Parish Unitarian Church (now known as First Church in Pembroke).

At the age of six, he entered the district school at Pembroke Center, and while not very good at math, in 1898, he passed the exams to enter high school. While in school, he studied Latin, French and Greek. In 1902, he passed the exams to enter Harvard College. He graduated Phi Beta Kappa with honors in 1907. His majors had been Latin, Greek, History, Philosophy and Government. In 1911, he left Harvard Graduate School with a PhD. He became an instructor in Latin and Greek at Harvard and Radcliffe and also was an associate professor of Latin at Amherst College. In 1915, illness forced him to retire to Pembroke, and he briefly taught Latin, history and French at Pembroke High School. Illness again forced him to give up teaching, and for many years, he toured the local vicinity on his bicycle, writing about the history of several of the local towns. After years of being in and out of hospitals and nursing homes, he passed away in a nursing home in Hanover. He was past ninety years of age.

For many years, he was a familiar figure around Pembroke. Toward the end of his life, he was usually dressed in his familiar black frock coat.

In 1974, D.J. Damkoehler wrote of Harry, "His character, intelligence, perseverance and native talent have made Henry Wheatland Litchfield the only 'landmark of Pembroke' that is missing from his book."

HIRAM RANDALL AND THE MAIL

If we look back at the history of mail delivery, it becomes apparent that the history of America might have been very different without a system of correspondence and "keeping in touch" with the widespread inhabitants of the original thirteen colonies.

The earliest European settlers of our area traveled from place to place along a network of Indian paths through the woods. They traveled either by foot, carrying packs on their backs, or by horseback with saddlebags. Frequently, the average traveler would carry with him a message or letter from one family to another. These messages might be passed on from traveler to traveler until they reached their final destination. It was not unusual for letters to arrive a full year after they had been written, if they arrived at all.

In 1718, a stage line was begun between Boston and Rhode Island, which may have been the first long-distance route. By the early 1800s, the number of stagecoaches had greatly increased, and the demand for better roads was created. The stagecoach lines were a greatly improved way to carry larger quantities of mail from one place to another.

Around 1810, a line of mail coaches ran between Boston, Plymouth and Sandwich. The stagecoaches left Boston on Tuesday, Thursday and Saturday mornings at 5:00 a.m. and made several stops along the way. On Monday, Wednesday and Friday mornings, they left Sandwich and made regular stops in reverse order. The stagecoach line ran through the towns of Dorchester, Quincy, Weymouth, Hingham, Scituate, Hanover, Pembroke, Duxbury, Kingston, Plymouth and on to Sandwich. For a person to travel from Boston all the way through to Sandwich on the mail coach cost $3.63. Eventually, the

Hiram Howland. *Pembroke Historical Society.*

Hiram Randall and Hiram Howland on the Hanover to Pembroke mail stage, circa 1895. *Pembroke Historical Society.*

development of rail transportation signaled the end of the mail stages in this part of the country, as it did the end of the Pony Express out west.

In the mid-1800s, Hiram Randall of West Duxbury began to transport the mail from his home on High Street by stagecoach to the railroad station at North Abington. He drove a four-horse tallyho coach and carried the mail from East, North and Center Pembroke. At this time, the mail for Pembroke Center was delivered to the post office located at the home of Seth Whitman on Barker Street. In 1883, Hiram Randall sold his stagecoach mail line to his son-in-law, Isaac Howland. Eventually, Isaac's son Hiram Howland (grandson of Hiram Randall) carried on the family mail stagecoach service, which was to remain in the same family for over one hundred years.

In 1916, Hiram Howland bought his first automobile to be used for mail delivery, bringing an end to the era of mail coaches in Pembroke.

Porter's Store

In the mid-1880s, Isaac Jennings built his Union Store, an old-fashioned country store at the intersection of Center and Mattakeesett Streets. In the typical nineteenth-century style, the store was filled with pickle and cracker barrels, cheese wheels and dry goods of all types.

Eventually, Jennings sold the store to Joseph Shepherd, who ran it with a partner. James Wilkenson left the business, and Shepherd operated it for several years by himself, but soon the building was empty. Sometime around 1900, Shepherd sold the business to Ira Franklin Porter, who was born in East Bridgewater in 1868, the son of farmer Cephas and Betsey (Drake) Porter.

In the 1900 U.S. census for the town of Pembroke, Ira F. Porter described himself as "a peddler of wholesale confections." I guess he was a kind of precursor to the old Cushman Bakery. Purchasing the building gave Ira a sense of stability and permanence, and in 1901, he married Bessie Haverstock of Duxbury. In 1910, Ira and Bessie were living in Middleborough with Ira's mother. Around 1913–14, a second story was added to the store, and Ira and Bessie moved into an upstairs apartment.

It appears that Ira continued his door-to-door sales for a time while Bessie ran the store. In 1938, the store was sold to Kenneth Henrich of Bryantville, who had worked for Ira and Bessie.

Joseph Shepherd, Ira and Bessie Porter and Kenneth Henrich were postmasters for Pembroke, and the store served as the post office until 1958

Ira Porter and his peddler's cart. *Pembroke Historical Society.*

when the post office was moved to a new building and Walter Erickson was appointed postmaster.

A fire in 1974 destroyed the building.

JAMES WEST, QUAKER

In the year 1846, a former North Pembroke Quaker set his pen to paper and began what he called "Sketches on Agricultural and Domestic Subjects Gathered from Observations and Other Sources" in an attempt to impart to future generations of his family and others his own brand of homespun wisdom on numerous subjects from how to prevent cold feet to how to keep cows from kicking.

His name was James West, and future generations of his family would become known in Pembroke as manufacturers of wooden boxes. James was born in 1804 in Randolph, Massachusetts, and died in 1890 in that part of Abington that is now part of Whitman. He was married to Hannah Ballard, and together they had nine children.

James was one of eight children born to parents who practiced the Calvinist faith. In an article he wrote for the *Boston Herald* about his religious conversions, he stated that he had "a small chance at a small district school, and not knowing the value of knowledge, made but a very poor use of the little chance I had." Until he was twenty-one, he spent his days farming and shoemaking, following the religious persuasions of his parents.

At the age of twenty-one, he became a Unitarian, still searching for religious meaning in his life. He studied hard but still felt unfulfilled in his quest to "satisfy his hungering soul." In the spring of 1840 or '41, after reading a little about Quakerism, he actually walked the fifteen miles from his home to the North Pembroke Quaker Meetinghouse. There he met Pembroke Quaker Calvin Shepherd, who helped guide him through some of the Quaker teachings. Eventually, he joined the meeting. Years later, still feeling a lack of spiritual connectedness, he began to read the writings of Emmanuel Swedenborg and "finally felt as never before, that the Lord is my great, kind, loving friend."

James West's great-great-great-grandson Richard West of Pembroke shared the homespun wisdom of this well-read, if little-educated, ancestor. Mr. West and I have enjoyed these rare glimpses into the life of a deeply devoted, hardworking gentleman of the nineteenth century.

What follows are some of Mr. West's tips to get you through the winter:

> *Odor for sick room—A few drops of oil of sandalwood dropped on a hot shovel is excellent for the air.*
>
> *To prevent cold feet—Draw off your stockings before undressing and rub feet and ankles with hands as hard as can be for five or ten minutes and you need not have cold feet in bed.*
>
> *How to cough—Keep straight and throw out the chest. This will expand the lungs and keep the windpipe free and clear, while the reverse posture serves to compress the lungs.*
>
> *Disordered stomach—Disordered stomachs, headaches and other slight indispositions are better and more readily cured by abstinence (from the food, but drink cold water) than by medicine.*
>
> *Remedy for cramp—Sleep in an inclined place, with the feet quite low, and gradually rising to the head, which should be pretty high.*
>
> *Diarrhea—Take rice water, salt to relish, and drink plentifully while warm.*
>
> *Warts and corns—Take the yoke of an egg, thicken it with fine salt, and apply as a poultice at night, having it off in the morning. This continue for two or three nights and the part affected bears a whitish appearance, then*

leave it off entirely. The wart or corn, it is said, will come out root and branch. If a little of the leaves of rye are bruised and added, it is said to be better.

For the activity of spring and summer gardening, Mr. West offers us the following advice:

> *Root Crops—require a rich soil, a dry soil, a deep soil and a well-pulverized soil. A good after culture will generally produce a good crop. Ashes should be applied.*
>
> *Potato Rot—Charcoal put in the hills, is said to prevent the rot, and put amongst potatoes in the spring, is said to prevent their sprouting or wilting.*
>
> *Compost—Fish oil, one barrel, will make 1½ or 2 cords of rich manure mixed with loam. It costs about 2 dollars a barrel and it is said to be the cheapest article for manure that can be bought.*
>
> *Coal as Manure—Bituminous coal ground to a fine powder, as fine as flour, is said to be the best fertilizer known, as it contains a large portion of carbon.*
>
> *Raising watermelons—Make the hills two feet high, six feet in circumference and place a barrel on the top of each hill and fill it with good manure. Plant the seeds on the outside of the barrel, all around it. Every morning, pour in a pail full of water. When the plants reach eight feet in length down the bottom of the hill, cover the ends over with soil.*
>
> *Peach trees—Soapsuds, ashes and salt spread around the roots kills the worms and improves the fruit.*
>
> *Times for seeding—Onions need to be sewn as soon as the ground will do to get a good crop, potatoes by the first of the fifth month, peas as soon as the ground will do and several times later. Parsnips, carrots and beets by the 25th of the 5th month, beans by the 20th of the 5th month, pumpkins, squashes, cucumbers and melons not before the 20th of the 5th month."*

(NOTE: Quakers never used the names for the months, as they believed them to be pagan. They were always referred to as the first month, fifth month and so forth.)

Give these tips a try—they just might lead you to your healthiest winter and your greatest garden ever!

And finally, some advice that is worth considering no matter what time of year:

Always busy—That's right, my lad. You will be something yet. I never knew a smart, active, industrious boy who did not turn out to be an energetic, enterprising and wealthy man. Better wear out than rust out, is a good proverb, and I rejoice to see it followed up. I would rather have you in my employ than a dozen downy-headed, sleeping, inactive youths, who do nothing from morning till night but heat the chair and read the newspapers.

JOSHUA CUSHING, AN EDUCATED MAN

One of the most important things to remember about local history, in my humble opinion, is that it is made up of the fabric woven with the stories of the lives of the people who chose to live there. With that in mind, I thought we'd take a look at some of the earliest families of Pembroke.

One such family is that of Joshua Cushing, Esquire. It is believed that Joshua was born in Scituate in 1670, the son of John and Sarah Cushing. In

The home of Joshua Cushing on Little's Avenue. *Pembroke Historical Society.*

1699, he married at Marshfield Mary Bacon, the daughter of Samuel and Mary Bacon. They were the parents of four children: Mary, Abigail, Joshua and Lydia. The family was living in Marshfield when, in January 1710, he purchased land at Mattakeesett (which later became Pembroke) from Robert Barker. His property was located on Little's Avenue near Allen Street.

An educated man, by the standards of that time, Joshua was chosen captain of the militia and also held a position on Pembroke's first board of selectmen. Local historian Harry Litchfield notes that although Joshua Cushing enjoyed an education that enabled him to serve as a justice, this same education "did not save him from diversifying our town records with strange phrases like 'One soar Blew Birds,' and his oft occurring [spelling] of 'Apeirll.'"

In addition to his position as selectman, Judge Cushing, as he was known, served as town clerk and the representative from Pembroke to the general court.

In 1725, he sold his seventy-three-acre Pembroke estate to his son-in-law Isaac Little of Marshfield.

In his book, *Ancient Landmarks of Pembroke*, Litchfield paints a picture of Judge Cushing as a righteous man who, along with his wife, "Madam Cushing," would invite visiting guests at their home to attend church services at the primitive First Church Meetinghouse. They would take their places in the family pew and sit in silent meditation as the Reverend Daniel Lewis preached. Eventually, the church deacons signaled the close of the service with the singing of the "Old Hundreth," and the Cushings and their guests would return to the Cushing home, where the men would discuss politics "flavored with stout cider from the Cushing orchard."

Joshua Cushing, it is believed, died at the home of his son in Kingston in 1750. It is unclear when and where his wife, Mary, died. Joshua is buried in Pembroke's Center Cemetery.

KILBORN WHITMAN

If you lived in Pembroke in the late eighteenth and early nineteenth centuries, you probably knew the name of Kilborn Whitman. Born in Bridgewater in 1765, he was the son of Zecheriah and Abigail (Kilborn) Whitman. He graduated from Harvard University in 1785 and studied for the ministry with the Reverend William Shaw of Marshfield. It was while he was at Marshfield that he met Elizabeth Winslow, a descendant of Governor Edward Winslow. Kilborn and Elizabeth were married at Marshfield in 1788.

Kilborn Whitman. *Pembroke Historical Society.*

He was called to the First Church in Pembroke as an assistant to the Reverend Thomas Smith in 1787, when Reverend Smith's eyesight was failing, and later became the church's third minister. A biographer described Reverend Whitman as "at first a Congregational but later a Unitarian in his beliefs. As a preacher he had fine presence, was forcible, elegant and popular."

By 1796, his family was increasing in number, and the constraints of a minister's salary caused him to retire from the ministry and begin the study of law with his brother Benjamin in Hanover. He was admitted to the bar in 1798 and attended courts in Plymouth, Bristol, Barnstable and Dukes Counties and the island of Nantucket. He kept his farm and home in Pembroke and had his office here. He served the town as a selectman, represented the town in the legislature, was an associate judge in the court of common pleas, was county attorney for Plymouth County and, with Judge Nymphas Marston of Barnstable, was overseer of the Mashpee and Herring Pond Indians, where, as their advocate, he conducted their business with "witty elegance and courtesy." He was considered "upright, dignified, able and urbane" by those who came in contact with him.

He frequently brought to his office law students to read law with him and was in high demand as a speaker for public banquets and dinners.

It is said that a frequent visitor to his Center Street home was the Honorable Daniel Webster, who, along with a large circle of friends, found there a cordial welcome, good conversation and generous hospitality.

The Reverend Judge Kilborn Whitman died in 1835, and his wife, Elizabeth, died in 1854. They are buried in Pembroke's Center Cemetery along with several of their eleven children.

Oliver's Story

Prior to the establishment of the Pembroke Almshouse (poor farm) in 1823, several systems were used to care for those individuals who were unable to provide for themselves. A committee appointed by the town, called Overseers of the Poor, was charged with finding reasonable lodging in the homes of local residents for those less fortunate. One system that was frequently used, especially to provide care for poor children, was a system of indenture, in which a young person was "bound out" to an individual who could provide basic necessities for the child as well as instruction in a trade. In return, the child would work for this individual for a specified period of time.

As I searched through the files of the Pembroke Historical Society for information on the care of the poor, I came across a folder that contained original indenture papers for several individuals. The terms to be fulfilled and the wording were about the same in each case, but one in particular caught my attention.

Oliver Grandison Healy (Heley) was born in Pembroke on October 17, 1813, the youngest of four children born to Reuben and Ruth (Magoun) Healy. Reuben had come to Pembroke from Vermont and married Ruth, the daughter of Abner and Ruth (Briggs) Magoun, in 1804. Oliver was only four when his mother died in 1817. The details of when and how the family came to their pauper circumstances are not immediately clear from the records. What is certain, however, is that in 1822, when Oliver was nine years of age, the Overseers of the Poor bound him out to Cornelius B. Magoun, his mother's brother. Cornelius was a shipwright, so we must assume that this was the trade young Oliver would eventually pursue.

The standard terms of indenture read as follows: "Said servant shall serve his said master faithfully and cause no damage to his said master. In all things and at all times, he shall behave as a good and faithful servant."

Oliver was to remain indentured to Mr. Magoun until October 17, 1829, when he was sixteen years of age. For his part, Cornelius Magoun was to "agree to teach and instruct the said servant or provide for his instruction in reading and writing and ciphering as far as the rule of three, as long as said servant is able to learn. He shall provide to said servant sufficient meat, drink and clothing and all other necessities fit and convenient for a servant. He shall give unto said servant two suits of wearing apparel, one suitable for the Lord's Day and the other suitable for working days."

Further information on Oliver was not readily available in the Pembroke records. Massachusetts vital records indicate that Oliver Healy and Phebe Reed married in Abington in 1834, and the 1850 U.S. census shows Oliver

G. Healy and his wife, Phebe, living in Abington. Oliver listed his occupation as "carpenter" and noted that he owned property valued at $6,000—not bad given his rough start in life. He died in 1876 in Abington of cholera morbus at the age of sixty-two. As harsh as this system seems today, it is interesting to note how important a reasonable education and vocational training were to our forefathers, in that even the poorest among them were given access to these basics for a successful future.

THE REVEREND DOCTOR GAD HITCHCOCK

Silhouette of the Reverend Dr. Gad Hitchcock. *Pembroke Historical Society.*

Not only does Pembroke have a wonderful legacy of historic events and antique homes, but it also has some particularly interesting people in its past. One such character was the Reverend Dr. Gad Hitchcock. Reverend Hitchcock was the first minister of the West Parish, which in 1820 became the town of Hanson.

The West Parish had been incorporated in 1746 from parts of Pembroke, Halifax, Hanover, Abington and Bridgewater. It was formed to give the residents of those areas better access to town and church meetings. A meetinghouse was built, and in 1748, Reverend Hitchcock was called. His ordination took place on the first Wednesday in October of that year. He was a native of Springfield, Massachusetts, where his ancestors had settled as early as 1644. He was born in 1719, graduated from Harvard College in 1743 and eventually received his doctorate of divinity from Harvard in 1787. He was married to Dorothy Angier of Cambridge, Massachusetts, who was connected with many old Cambridge families. Their only son, Dr. Gad Hitchcock, also a graduate of Harvard College, became the first medical doctor to settle in the parish.

Reverend Hitchcock is probably best known for an election sermon that he was invited to give before Governor Gage and the House of Representatives on May 25, 1774. The text of his sermon came from Proverbs 29:2; his theme was "The Reign of the Wicked." He had not planned for Governor Gage to actually be in attendance, but he was. His friends begged him to change his sermon, but Reverend Hitchcock refused. Needless to say, the governor was not pleased, but apparently, many of the members of the House of Representatives were sympathetic to the colonial cause, for they sent him a thank-you document along with a request for a copy of the sermon, which would be given to the press. It is also believed that he was sent the gift of a suit of clothes from the House clerk, Samuel Adams.

The Reverend Dr. Gad Hitchcock sometimes served as chaplain during the American Revolution and is said to have served with great bravery.

The home of the Reverend Dr. Gad Hitchcock in the West Parish of Pembroke, now Hanson. *Pembroke Historical Society.*

He was also a member of the convention that framed the Massachusetts Constitution in 1780.

The Reverend Dr. Gad Hitchcock ministered to the people of the West Parish for more than fifty-five years. In November 1802, the Reverend George Barstow was called to carry on the work of Hitchcock's ministry, as Gad had become too infirm to preach to the people. Gad Hitchcock Sr. died in August 1803.

Josiah Smith, United States Congressman

Many times over the years, I've talked about how much history you can learn just by taking a walk in an old cemetery on a warm day and reading some of the epitaphs. Recently, while taking advantage of the beautiful early spring warmth, I took a walk through the old part of our Center Cemetery looking for the ancestors of a lady from Texas who had written to me. The old cemetery did not disappoint me.

Among the lichen-covered stones was one that was broken completely down the middle but with an epitaph clearly readable: "Erected to the Memory of the Hon. Josiah Smith Esq. late member of the Congress of the United States who died April ye 4th 1803 Aged 66 years." OK, I thought. This was worth further investigation.

Josiah Smith was the second of twelve children born to the Reverend Thomas Smith and his wife, Judith (Miller) Smith. Thomas was the second minister of First Church in Pembroke. While Josiah's official congressional biography states that he was born in Pembroke on February 26, 1738, his father was still the minister at Yarmouth, Massachusetts, at that time and did not move with his family to Pembroke until 1754, when he was hired by First Church, so it seems he was probably born in Yarmouth. In 1760, he married Mary Barker, daughter of Elisha and Elizabeth (Bowen) Barker, and his second cousin. He served as a deacon at First Church, and the couple's eleven children were born in Pembroke.

Josiah was a graduate of Harvard College in 1774. He studied law and was admitted to the bar and practiced locally. Also, in 1774, two years after the Pembroke Resolves were written, he was chosen as one of the members of the committee from Pembroke who reported to the committee of correspondence the approval of our town of the actions of the various colonies: "Resolved, that we will, at the risk of our lives and fortunes, in every

The gravestone of the Honorable Josiah Smith, Esquire, in Pembroke's Center Cemetery. *Photo by John Proctor.*

justifiable method, assert and defend our just rights and privileges as men and colonists." Later, in 1789 and 1790, he was a member of the Massachusetts State House of Representatives. From 1792 to 1794 and again in 1797, he served in the state senate. In 1797, he became state treasurer.

On March 4, 1801, he was elected as a Republican to the Seventh Congress of the United States, where he served until March 3, 1803. On April 4, 1803, Josiah Smith died in Pembroke of a disease he had contracted while in Washington, D.C.

Several sons of Josiah Smith operated the Smith Ship Yard on the North River until 1819. The names of many of the descendants of the Smith family appear prominently in Pembroke town records since these early times. Susan A. Smith, a descendant of this family, was a prolific writer and recorder of Pembroke history, and her writings are frequently referenced today by this writer and others.

Local Historians and Their Writings

In any town with a history as significant as Pembroke's, you can usually find any number of history buffs, eager to give you their own personal "slant" on the events that shaped the area in which they live. Harry W. Litchfield, a Pembroke native and eminent Harvard professor of philosophy, is one whose writings are turned to again and again by those of us who are fascinated with the local past. Among his writings was a brief list and description of those Pembroke residents he felt had made a significant contribution to our knowledge of Pembroke's past.

The first person on Litchfield's list is the Reverend Morrill Allen, fifth pastor of First Church in Pembroke who gave, in the year 1850, an impressive sermon on community history that Litchfield used in his book, *Ancient Landmarks of Pembroke*.

Second on the Litchfield list is Dr. Francis Collamore, a physician at North Pembroke, who, in 1883, wrote a general history of the town for Hurd's *History of Plymouth County*.

Jane (Gurney) Bryant, wife of William Henry Harrison Bryant, left us manuscripts on King Phillip's path as it wound south of Little Sandy Pond to Mattakeesett Way and Barker Street. Her research was carried on between 1890 and 1900.

Susan A. Smith (1847–1920) of North Pembroke—whose roots go back to the second minister of First Church in Pembroke, the Reverend Thomas

Susan Augusta Smith. *Pembroke Historical Society.*

Smith—compiled a history of the town of Pembroke from the records of the town clerk in 1895.

Another favorite local historian whose writings are greatly respected is Sarah Elizabeth (White) Bosworth. She was born at South Marshfield, the daughter of Thomas White. She married Henry Bosworth of Pembroke and lived at the ancestral Bosworth home on Center Street near Mountain

George Lewis and his wife, Marion (Keene) Lewis. *Pembroke Historical Society.*

Avenue. She was a teacher and noted public speaker whose interest was in military history. She was best known for her article "Pembroke in the Civil War" and a number of family genealogy manuscripts.

George Edward Lewis, a printer, is called by Litchfield a "picture historian" who began printing postcards around 1900 and was the printer of the *Bryantville News* in which he co-authored many articles.

Mercer V. Tillson, a foundryman from the Bryantville area, is credited with definitively locating Pembroke's section of the Bay Path, the ancient main route from Boston to Plymouth.

William W. Bryant wrote many articles on the local Native Americans for the *Bryantville News*, as well as articles on the Acadians.

Anne (Bonney) Henderson, in addition to sundry maps and articles about Norwell, drew an excellent historic map of Pembroke showing locations of the first houses in our area.

It is interesting to note the variety of people, men and women, and their diverse professions. Their efforts involved pure research, hours of poring over original documents, old letters and town records in an effort to make easier the lives of those of us who came later and had an interest in our historic past. Each time I sit down to write about our town, I am reminded of their efforts, and I am very grateful.

PEMBROKE'S PIONEERS

When we think of the word "pioneer" we tend to think of this westward expansion period of our history, but the dictionary defines pioneer as "one of the first to settle in a territory." Using this definition, we can trace the pioneering spirit back to our own town of Pembroke and to a group who, in the 1780s, set off for new territory—in Maine.

According to *The History of Sumner, Maine*, families from Pembroke, Massachusetts—named Bonney, Bisbee, Briggs, Cole, Hollis, Hayford, Robinson, Stetson, Tillson, Oldham, Ford and Keene—moved to what was then known as East and West Butterfield, or Butterfield Plantation, Maine. Most had been given one hundred acres of land or soldiers' notes by the government as payment for their military service in the Revolutionary War. The notes had little value in Massachusetts but were able to be used at their full value to purchase land in the district of Maine. (Maine was part of Massachusetts until 1820.)

The first Pembroke family to settle in this new place in the wilderness was the family of Daniel or David Oldham (there is some discrepancy in the records about Mr. Oldham's first name). Next came the family of Charles Ford and then the family of William Hayford. These families established farms on their new land.

In 1783, the family of Increase Robinson arrived and, the next season, built the first sawmill and then the first frame house in the area. That year, Charles Bisbee arrived from Pembroke on a sailing vessel, landing first at Freeport, Maine, and then loading his possessions on two horses for the inland trek to the Butterfield area.

By 1798, the Butterfield Plantation had split to become the towns of Sumner and Hartford, Maine. By then, these first families from Pembroke had been joined by families from other locations (mostly in Massachusetts) to populate and develop this new, burgeoning frontier.

Not all Pembroke-area pioneers to Maine were driven by the promise of land. Some moved there to join growing communities of the Quaker faith, such as Vassalborough and Unity, Maine. Other towns in Maine were also populated by Pembroke residents. Members of one branch of the Barker family, first settlers of Pembroke, found their way to Dresden, Skowhegan and Norridgewock, Maine.

PEMBROKE'S LOYALISTS

Each year as the month of April rolls around, besides the thoughts of warmer weather and the Boston Marathon, my mind wanders back to the historic events of another April, back in 1775, when events in Massachusetts forever changed the way people could, if they chose, be governed in countries all over the world.

In the past, I've written about those Patriots from Pembroke who left their homes to fight for our freedoms—you know, those brave citizens whose names are emblazoned on monuments in public places all over town.

Recently, while researching another subject, I came across the names of four Pembroke residents whose names will probably never be on any monuments except, perhaps, their gravestones. In the book *Divided Hearts, Massachusetts Loyalists 1765–1790: A Biographical Directory*, compiled and edited by David E. Maas, appear the names of Prince Barker, Samuel House, Isaiah Josselyn and Thomas Josselyn Jr., all of Pembroke, who, for whatever reason, chose the side of the British over the side of the Patriots in the American Revolutionary War.

In 1774, British authority virtually collapsed in areas outside Boston, and those who found themselves on the wrong side of the argument found their lives becoming intolerable. The growing angry sentiments of the Patriots subjected the Loyalists to scathing personal abuse. More and more, Loyalists from outlying areas fled to Boston and the protection of the British troops stationed there. By 1776, the British army had abandoned Boston, and many, but not all, adult male Loyalists fled as well to places like Nova Scotia and London.

The Loyalists, however, did not stay away. Between 1775 and 1782, over half of the Loyalists who left Massachusetts returned either by force or voluntarily. According to Maas's research, all four of the aforementioned Pembroke Loyalists remained in Massachusetts after the British departed. They were all found guilty in an inimical trial in 1777. Samuel House, who in September 1776 had been "warned" by Sergeant Elisha Record by order of Lieutenant Nathaniel Thomas to appear at Captain Josiah Cushing Jr.'s at one o'clock in the afternoon for the conflict at arms, was named in the records as a husbandman and was jailed in 1777. Thomas Josselyn Jr., named in the records as a farmer, was jailed in 1775–76. In the book *The Loyalists of Massachusetts*, the description of Thomas Josselyn Jr. reads, "Of Pembroke, an 'infamous Tory,' stubborn, refractory and evasive." Prince Barker was listed as a yeoman and a Quaker and does not appear from the records to have served time in jail. He died in 1784 and is buried in the cemetery at the Friends Meetinghouse in Pembroke. Isaiah Josselyn, named in the records as a yeoman, also does not appear to have been jailed. Isaiah was probably a resident of that part of Pembroke that became Hanson in 1820.

WHAT'S IN A NAME?

"A rose by any other name would smell as sweet." These words were made famous by the Bard of Avon, William Shakespeare, four centuries ago. Yet, rich or poor, famous or infamous, the one thing every parent has to give freely to a child is his or her "good name." As I watched my children and their spouses take on the challenge of finding the perfect names for my grandchildren, I was reminded again of the awesome task of giving name to a new life.

First names, Christian names or given names, whatever one chooses to call them, tend to go through cycles, and it seems to be that girls' names tend to be more "original," if you will, than boys' names. A number of years ago, for example, there was a run on girls' names ending in the letter *i*.

Historically, our ancestors had fewer resources for picking their children's names than we do today. They expressed their creativity by taking the more unusual route. While family names were often used, by far, the most common source of names for children in the seventeenth, eighteenth and nineteenth centuries was the Bible. After all, few people in those days had access to a variety of books, but practically every household had a Bible. Even if no one in the family could read, listening to three- or four-hour sermons every Sunday certainly acquainted one with biblical contents. Although the names of the Apostles were frequently chosen, many parents appeared to look for the more uncommon biblical references when choosing a name. Perhaps this was done because the

An unidentified Pembroke baby, proving that names are important. *Pembroke Historical Society.*

parents hoped that their child would take on some of the qualities exhibited by their namesakes in the "Good Book."

Looking through the births section of the vital records of Pembroke to the year 1850, I came across some wonderful old biblical names that we don't hear much anymore outside a church or temple. A friend loaned me a book that describes each biblical character in some detail, so I decided to see what I could find.

The early Delano family of Pembroke named one of their sons Zebedee, probably after the biblical character who was the father of apostles James and John and the husband of Salome. Certainly that man was doing something right! Several in the Keen family were named Lazarus, after the man who was resurrected from the dead by Jesus. An admirable sort, no doubt.

Now, I'm not so sure about the reason the Bourn family named their daughter Tamar. After all, one biblical Tamar pretended to be a harlot in order to trick Judah, while another biblical Tamar was a rape victim. I'm also not so sure why the early Bisbe family named their daughter Rizpah. This biblical character was a concubine of King Saul.

I must admit that I was rather tickled by the names Eleazar and Lydia Hamlen of Pembroke gave their rather large brood in the 1750s and 1760s. Four of their eight children were named Africa, America, Asia and Europe. Apparently they were more interested in impressing friends and family with their knowledge of geography than with their knowledge of the Bible. Their worldly awareness seems to have stopped there because their other four children were named Alice, Cyrus, Betsey and Lydia.

But my heart goes out to the son of Jacob and Kizea Barstow, born in Pembroke in 1768, who had to go through life saddled with the name Burden.

Part IV

HOLIDAYS AND OTHER DAYS

An Early Twentieth-Century Fourth of July

Parades, cookouts, picnics, trips to the beach or the local park and sparklers all culminated with the annual municipal fireworks display—these are the sights and sounds of a modern-day Fourth of July celebration. Historically, this was the first, the original, American holiday. On July 4, 1776, sounds of bells ringing floated over the city of Philadelphia, calling the people to gather at what would become known as Independence Hall to hear the reading of the new Declaration of Independence. Some historians claim that there are no actual records indicating that it was the Liberty Bell that rang for all to hear; others say that since it was the loudest bell in Philadelphia, it must have been the one ringing on that historic day. It was not until two days later, on July 6, 1776, that news of the signing of the declaration reached Boston. Soldiers fired their cannons thirteen times in honor of the thirteen new American states, drums beat and bells rang. Bonfires were lit, fueled by signs proclaiming allegiance to King George as people danced around singing patriotic songs. John Adams proclaimed that the day the Continental Congress voted for independence should be celebrated forever. He believed America's birthday should be marked with parades, shows, games, sports, guns, bells and bonfires. Although America still had to fight a long war with England, the people still found the time to celebrate the Fourth of July by building bonfires, shooting guns and ringing bells.

Undoubtedly, the home of the first expression in favor of a war for American Independence (known historically as the Pembroke Resolves), Pembroke, Massachusetts, held similar celebrations. While records of the earliest Fourths of July in Pembroke are virtually nonexistent, the *Bryantville News* gives us a sense of how we celebrated this important day at the turn of the century. You will note that what had become a traditional event, the ringing of church bells all over the nation at noon on the Fourth, was honored in Pembroke:

> *The "Fourth" in Bryantville was ushered in this year* [1905] *with much less noise than of former years. There was no band and the squad of boys that paraded the street just after twelve, was conspicuous by their absence. Lewis and Turner's store seemed to be headquarters as usual and all night long they were kept busy waiting upon customers, and before the dawn their large stock of fireworks was nearly all sold out. The boys built two or three fires in the streets but no vandalism of any sort was carried out. There were two or three persons of the masculine gender whose enthusiasm got the better of them…but they were promptly offered a night's lodging at the lock up at* [Mayflower] *Grove.*
>
> *Of course, the church bells were rung, and all thoroughly enjoyed themselves in a quiet way.*

APRIL 19, 1776

Historically speaking, the month of April in Massachusetts is significant for its commemoration of Patriots Day, April 19. Every so often, I like to remind today's residents of Pembroke of the story of our American Partriots—those who answered the call of freedom during a difficult yet historically glorious time in American history. They were an example for people all over the world to use as a model for their own people's revolts against tyrannical governments.

Pembroke's activities on behalf of the cause of American freedom, of course, actually began years before April 18 and 19, 1775, with the issue of the Pembroke Resolves in 1772 calling for separation from the mother country, England. So when the "Lexington Alarm" sounded, men from towns and cities all over the colony of Massachusetts, including Pembroke, gathered into their local militia companies and prepared to march toward headquarters in Cambridge and eventually, if necessary, on to Lexington and the almost simultaneous battle at Concord. All in all, more than twenty thousand "embattled farmers" answered the call to arms.

The muster rolls of the April 19 mobilization are housed at the Massachusetts State Archives at Columbia Point and, while not quite complete, offer a good picture of what happened that day and who was involved.

- The town of Pembroke sent troops as follows:
- 49 men under the command of Freedom Chamberlain
- 62 regular militiamen under the command of Elijah Cushing
- 53 minutemen under the command of James Hatch
- 74 regular militiamen under the command of Thomas Turner

for a total of 238 men.

In actuality, only one-seventh of the approximately twenty thousand men took part in the fighting on April 19, but each and every one of them answered the call. The militia system in Massachusetts, although well prepared to confront the British in terms of drill and spirit, was somewhat lacking in terms of organization. Ready or not, however, on April 19, 1775, the militia system was in action.

Early local historian Susan Smith noted that the town of Pembroke stands preeminent as having sent more soldiers (500) according to its size (1,500 residents) than any other town over the course of the years during which the War for American Independence was fought. Thanks to the late, much-beloved Pembroke resident Everett Reed, a listing of all the men from Pembroke who served can be seen on plaques located in Veterans' Memorial Hall on the lower level at town hall.

BACK TO SCHOOL

Each late August or early September, hoards of parents and children head to the shopping malls all over the South Shore for the "necessities" of school life for the next nine or so months. I thought it might be interesting to look at the items for sale in August and September one hundred years ago. I turned to the pages of the *Bryantville News*, published around 1903, for answers.

As you can imagine, times have changed. You could buy the latest styles and tints of paper for twenty-five cents per pound, as well as pens, pencils, inks and mucilage at the stationery department of F.H. Gurney of Whitman, Massachusetts. Fall-style hats, school suits and shoes could be purchased at Johnson's of Whitman. Miss Porter, also of Whitman, had the new fall ginghams, outing flannels and flannelettes for sewing back-to-school outfits for the thrifty.

Lewis and Turner, Grocers, offered the best meats and groceries, and the Cushman Bakery had a large assortment of cakes, pies and other baked goods for those hearty school lunches.

Other than the above-listed items, there was very little mention of the need to purchase the latest, biggest or most expensive (but on sale) merchandise so your child could have the right equipment for a successful school year.

So…what has changed in one hundred years? Merchandising obviously has progressed by leaps and bounds. And, of course, our needs have changed—I wonder what a parent from 1900 would think about what our students need today? We have become a more creative (hence the need for crayons, aka art supplies), technology-savvy (hence the need for everything else) society. Did the students of one hundred years ago require the latest fashions, or perhaps a better question—would they be allowed to wear the latest fashions to the classroom? The sum total of their technological needs seems to have been a pencil, a pen and some fresh, clean paper and perhaps some scissors and a little glue to hold everything together.

Now, I don't know of anybody, including myself, who longs for the "good old days," but this is the kind of research that makes me go, "Hmmmmm."

AN EIGHTEENTH-CENTURY COUNTRY WEDDING

A few years ago, I found an article in the *Bryantville News* that was published in 1912. It was written in 1837 by Julia Collamore, daughter of Horace Collamore of Pembroke. Julia had been told the story by her grandmother Laurentia (Hall) Briggs just a few days before Mrs. Briggs's death in 1837. It is believed to be an account of Laurentia's own wedding to Elisha Briggs on November 20, 1777. It is a wonderful example of how family stories, passed from generation to generation, while not always perfectly accurate, can give us a glimpse of what life in historic Pembroke was truly like. The story goes as follows, in Julia's own words:

> *About a century ago, there lived a wealthy man who had several daughters. With the prospects of one, he was much pleased, and therefore gave what was called in those days, a splendid wedding. He lived in a low house,*

situated on rising ground, built of large oak timbers, stout and strong. The chimneys were large and burned large logs that took two men to carry, instead of splitting the wood fine, as they now do.

There was a large orchard near the house that contained very large trees and other large trees were in front of the house. The floors were all white and had no carpets on them. The walls were neither plastered nor papered, but were all boarded without being painted.

As there were so many boards to be kept clean, they were not scoured very frequently, but on such an occasion as this, every crack and corner must be made as nice as possible.

Thus, after having scoured their house and sanded their floors, they prepared their poultry and hung them up in readiness to cook for the feast. The guests, composed of all their acquaintances, neighbors and relatives, having assembled, the ceremony commenced.

The bride was dressed in a new silk robe and white linen apron, which she had spun and woven herself. She wore a white silk cap trimmed with bright red ribbon (which seems to have been a favorite color at that time) and gold beads tied around her neck.

The minister performed the ceremony after which the newly married couple was obliged to keep standing until all the gentlemen present had saluted the bride with a kiss, and the ladies the bridegroom in the same manner.

Then, to close the wedding they had a dance, and all those who could not dance would take turns singing.

FROM LADIES' FAIR TO OLD HOME DAYS

It is an event that occurs every year in small towns throughout America and especially in New England: the annual church fair. Its roots go back in history to a time unknown, perhaps as far back as the English Druids. The beginnings of the American church fair, however, are much newer. Our Puritan forefathers were deeply rooted in the more pious ways of providing money for church activities—tithing, where each church family was expected to give 10 percent of its income to the church, and taxation, where everybody in the community paid for the support and care of the church and the minister whether or not they were part of the church. Eventually, with the belief in separation of church and state, taxation was no longer a means by which the church could provide for its needs. Tithing was often difficult for families, and weekly offerings could vary greatly from season to season, a victim of weather and crop success or failure. While many local churches had larger parent organizations to provide some assistance, the New England Congregational churches were completely autonomous, relying solely on their members for support.

The First Church in Pembroke began in 1712 as a direct offshoot of the Puritan church. In fact, many of its original members were direct descendants of the "first comers," or Pilgrims, as they were also known. It was founded as a direct result of the colonial Massachusetts law that stated that a community must have an established church in order to be recognized as an incorporated town. So, the survival of the town was totally dependent on the factors mentioned earlier.

Over the years, as the Puritan influence declined, newer ways were needed to help finance the church's needs. The annals of First Church in Pembroke begin to show "ladies' fairs" that actually provided the money for such things as fences around Center Cemetery, in addition to the regular work of the church. Farmers donated produce, and women gave handmade quilts and garments as well as baked goods to be sold, the proceeds of which went to the church.

Center Cemetery fence funded largely by the First Parish Sewing Circle's Ladies' Fairs. *Photo by John Proctor.*

Browsing the homemade goods at the fair in the 1960s. *First Church in Pembroke.*

During the 1960s, it was discovered that the proceeds of these fairs would not cover all the expenses of a growing church family, much less the wider mission of the church to help others in need. This was the start of a larger "Old Home Days Fair" that included rides and games. While some mourned the loss of the simpler church fair held each spring, others believed there was a need for a more profitable means of attracting financial help for the church.

Today, those of us who enjoy the historical and local charm of the small fair can still enjoy this atmosphere in the Harvest Fair—not only does it help to provide much-needed money to continue the church's work, but it is also truly a look back to one of the charming traditions of our New England Congregational church.

Dearly Departed

I've always thought that the month of October was one of the most beautiful months of the year. As a child, I looked forward to its arrival because it signaled that my birthday was close at hand. As I grew older, I began to appreciate the crisp, cool, clear days and nights—"October's bright blue weather," as one poet described it.

October culminates in the celebration of All Saints' Eve or Halloween (Hallowed Eve) by some Christian denominations. Today, the emphasis on costumes and celebrations of trick or treat hearken back to the holiday's even earlier pagan roots. The dying back of plant life and the preparation for the long, cold winter have caused October to be viewed as a month when death is, if not celebrated, then at least honored.

With that said, I decided to write a bit about long-forgotten death rituals—called part of the rites of passage by some. From early times until

A fine example of hair jewelry on display at the Pembroke Historical Society. *Photo by John Proctor.*

the dawn of the twentieth century, funeral services were held in the home. From the Middle Ages to the colonial period of our history, custom required that the family of the deceased give mourning rings or gloves to mourners, and money was often set aside in the deceased's will for such expenditures. Mourning rings often had a small receptacle in which to place a lock of the dearly departed's hair.

In the 1850s, women began to make jewelry out of the deceased person's hair. The hair could be woven into brooches, bracelets, watch chains and earrings. While not used exclusively for mourning, hair jewelry seemed a natural way to remember a loved one. Examples of mourning jewelry can be found in many museums.

In the 1860s, black drapes were hung around the house of the family of the deceased, and a widow was required by custom to wear black clothing for at least one year after her husband's death.

Funeral cards, which originally were used to invite mourners to the funeral; large mausoleums in park-like cemeteries; and postmortem photographs of the deceased in his or her coffin were also popular visual reminders of the dearly departed.

These ritualistic behaviors seem rather peculiar to most of us today. Today, we seem to concentrate on celebrating the life of the deceased, often placing balloons, toys and small reminders of a person's life at the grave site rather than focusing on the darker acts of mourning. However one remembers a loved one in death, these rituals and rites of passage will probably continue to change and evolve as we travel through this century and beyond.

Part V

SACRED PLACES AND MEMORIALS

Briggs Burial Ground

You can learn a lot about a town's history by studying the lives of the people who came before us. Epitaphs can give you a glimpse into the minds and hearts of our rugged forebears; dates of births and deaths can point to epidemics or other tragedies that befell our towns in those earliest years.

One cemetery in town that is quite interesting is the Briggs Burying Ground on Washington Street. Before it was turned over to the town for care late in the last century, the cemetery was in trust for the descendants of its namesake, Seth Briggs, who was born in 1721 and died in 1801. Historically, it has also been known as the Barker Burial Ground and the Burying Hill. According to late Pembroke historian Alton Ford, at the top of the hill and back over the fence is a hollow near which some of the slaves of Pembroke's earliest residents are buried. Just inside the fence on the right is the location of the old North Pembroke schoolhouse, which was moved many years ago when a group of children playing near the school accidentally began to unearth one of the bodies.

The Barkers, Pembroke's first family, buried several of their children there between 1722 and 1729. Two of the children of Thomas and Bethia Barker—Elizabeth, age two, and Nathaniel, age six—were both interred in November 1722 within two days of each other, which could signify an outbreak of smallpox, dysentery, cholera or some other awful sickness.

Gravestone of Mr. Seth Briggs Jr. *Pembroke Historical Society.*

The burial ground also is the final resting place of one of Pembroke's more illustrious citizens: nationally renowned architect Alexander Parris, who died in 1852 after creating such buildings as First Church in Pembroke, Bunker Hill Monument, Charlestown Navy Yard and the treasury building in Washington, D.C.—just to name a few.

Other people like Ichabod Thomas and Benjamin Turner, both Pembroke shipbuilders on the North River, are buried there. The *Maria*, the ship

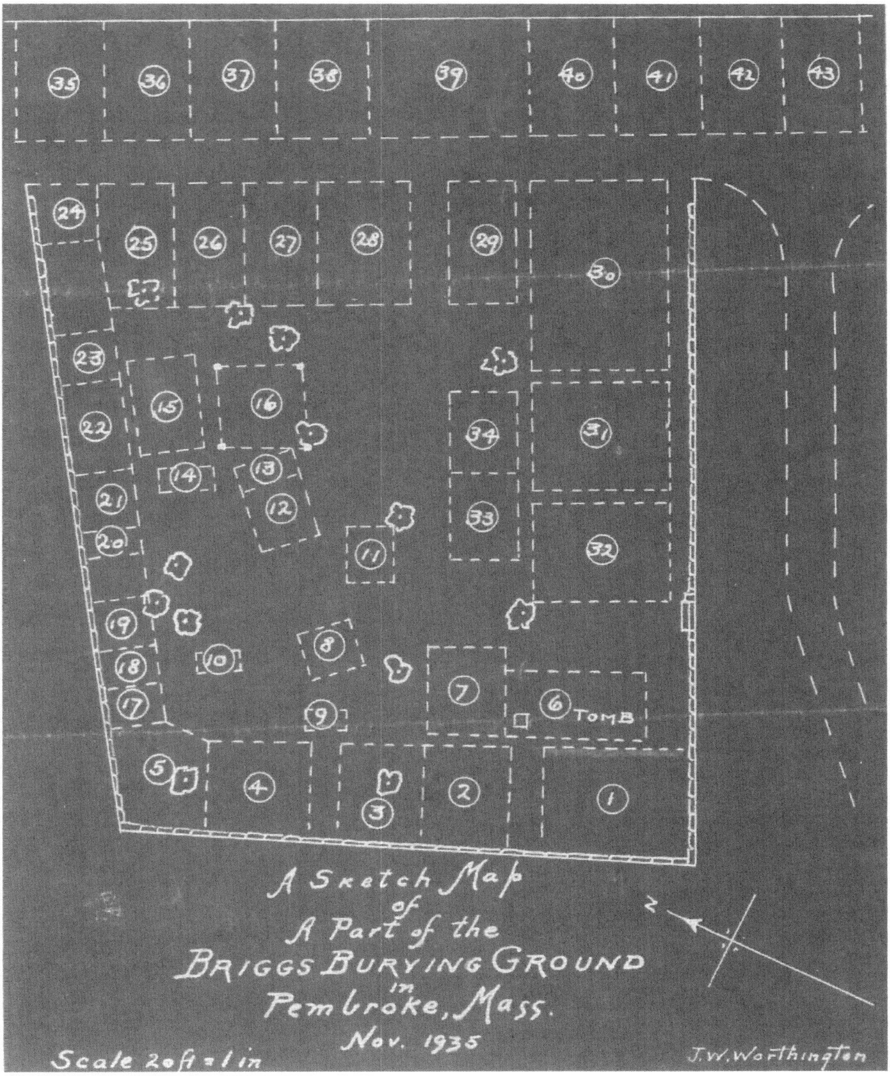

Map of Briggs Burying Ground. *Pembroke Historical Society.*

depicted on Pembroke's town seal, was built by Ichabod Thomas at the Brick Kiln shipyard, one of the North River's most prolific yards.

The list of other burials in the Briggs Burial Ground reads like a who's-who of eighteenth- and nineteenth-century Pembroke: Cushing, Collamore, Simmons, Ford—just to name a few. Sometimes, all that these individuals left behind of their lives is "written in stone."

THE CENTER CEMETERY

Most of us drive by it several times a day without giving it much attention. However, at the time of year known as Halloween, with the trimmings and trappings revolving around black cats, ghosts, goblins and tombstones etched with RIP, suddenly the town cemetery becomes the inspiration for all the good-natured fun. Few of us think of it as an excellent example of local history in its purest form.

A walk through Pembroke's Center Cemetery is truly a step back in time. Each of the inhabitants once lived, loved and died in Pembroke, making the town, even in a small way, what it is today. The names on the stones read like a street directory of Pembroke. There are Dwelleys, Bryants, Barkers, Oldhams, Littles—the list goes on and on. The cemetery is the final resting place for the poor dirt farmer and the wealthy shipbuilder, as well as the noted composer and the respected local clergyman.

It is difficult to know exactly when the first grave was made. So many of the oldest stones are long gone—victims of weather and air pollution. The late local historian Harry Litchfield noted that in 1909 the earliest readable stone was that of a child of Isaac Thomas who died on August 28, 1715. The oldest stones are located in the northeastern corner of the cemetery, near the church.

Pembroke's Center Cemetery, showing First Church in the background. *Pembroke Historical Society.*

Center Cemetery's wrought-iron gate. *Photo by John Proctor.*

For well over one hundred years, the cemetery was controlled by the First Parish or Precinct of Pembroke. By 1833, the Town of Pembroke had taken over most of the maintenance duties, and the "First Parish Burying Ground" became the "Common Burying Ground." (The Association for Gravestone Studies defines the difference between a burying ground and a cemetery by age. A "burying ground" is an early cemetery. It was the term used during the seventeenth and eighteenth centuries as a place of burial while "cemetery" is the term used beginning in the nineteenth century.)

Over the years, there have been a number of fences and stone walls erected around the perimeter of the cemetery. The first was a crude wooden structure put in place in 1807. In 1852, it was voted to allow the proceeds of the Ladies' Fair held by the First Parish Sewing Circle, in addition to an appropriate sum of money from the surplus revenue fund to be spent on a stone post fence with iron rails to be built on the north and east boundaries of the cemetery.

Like so many other sites of local historic interest, the Center Cemetery has many notable features. Harry McGregor Woods, composer of such tunes as "When the Red, Red Robin Comes Bob, Bob, Bobbin' Along" and a former Pembroke resident, is buried here. The Center Cemetery is a repository for several cast-iron gravestones. Very few of these markers exist in New

England, and their origin is not truly known. Lastly, there is a favorite legend of mine relating to the late Reverend Morrill Allen, fifth minister of the First Church in Pembroke. Reverend Allen was deeply concerned with the character of those ministers who would follow him. Prior to his death in 1870, he carefully chose the location of his final resting place. He saw to it that every successive minister who gazed out the windows of the church while at the pulpit delivering their sermon would look directly at the headstone of the Reverend Allen. In turn, Reverend Allen would be forever watching them—something for future ministers of First Church to think about.

A CENOTAPH FOR CHRISTOPHER SMITH?

Behind a home on West Elm Street, on land once owned by members of early Pembroke's Smith family, is a small patch of ground surrounded by granite blocks. Carved in one of the blocks is the name Christopher Smith with the dates December 22, 1757, and July 10, 1781. Christopher was the

Full view of the probable cenotaph for Christopher Smith on West Elm Street. *Photo by John Proctor.*

twelfth child of the Reverend Thomas Smith and his wife, Judith (Miller) Smith. The Reverend Thomas Smith was born at Yarmouth and was himself the ninth of thirteen children. Thomas graduated from Harvard College in 1725, was ordained as a minister in 1729 and married Judith Miller in 1734. Thomas ministered at the Yarmouth church for twenty-five years, but his religious views were becoming too liberal for his congregation. He seemed to be a welcome relief to Pembroke's First Church congregation after the ministry of Daniel Lewis. So in 1754, about a year after Lewis's death, Smith came to Pembroke, built a gambrel-roofed home on Center Street and became the second minister of the First Church in Pembroke.

It was during Smith's ministry that the events leading to the American Revolution took place, including the drafting of the famous "Pembroke Resolves," which warned the English king that the colonists were ready to fight for their rights. Although a staunch Patriot, Lewis had reached the advanced age of seventy and had lost some of his youthful enthusiasm for the cause. It was actually the younger minister of the West Parish of Pembroke, Gad Hitchcock, who led the townspeople through those turbulent times.

It was also during this time that Thomas's youngest son, Christopher Smith, served in Captain Thomas Turner's militia company that responded

A close-up of the engraving on the cenotaph. *Pembroke Historical Society.*

to the alarm on April 19, 1775. He later served in Captain Freedom Chamberlain's company when it marched on Dorchester Heights on March 6, 1776. He also served with Captain John Turner's company on September 28, 1777, on their march to Rhode Island.

It seems that Christopher did not die as a direct result of this military service. After the abovementioned service, he "followed the sea" and was last heard from aboard an English prison ship at Halifax, Nova Scotia, where Christopher died in 1781 at the age of twenty-four. Although local historians sometimes disagree, I have found no positive proof that Christopher Smith is actually buried within these walls. In my opinion, it seems rather unlikely. Christopher died very far from home during a time when travel was long and arduous and the political climate tumultuous. Had his remains been returned to Pembroke, being the son of a minister, surely he would have been buried in the sacred ground of the Center Cemetery near his parents and many of his brothers and sisters. The enclosure on West Elm Street most likely stands as a monument to a beloved son by a proud but grieving family.

The Civil War Monument

Memorial Day and the Fourth of July—summertime holidays, yes, but also two good reasons to reflect on all those who fought and especially those who gave their lives in defense of our nation. Memorial Day festivities often get me thinking about the Civil War Monument on the town green—what it represents and how it got there.

After the conclusion of the Civil War, veterans' groups like the GAR began to spring up throughout the northern states. Pembroke's veterans began meeting on a regular basis in the year 1869. These first meetings were held at Mechanics Hall on High Street (now the High Street fire station). By 1896, the group moved its meetings to the newly erected GAR Hall, now the Police Boys' Club.

It was during this postwar period that some Pembroke residents felt it important to build a monument dedicated to the Civil War soldiers. A "Monument Association" first met in July 1879. It held an election of officers to include Dr. Francis Collamore as president and Miles Sampson, William H.H. Bryant, Mr. and Mrs. George H. Mann and Clara M. Bonney as vice-presidents. George H. Ryder was elected treasurer. They also elected a large executive committee, several of whom died before the plans

The Civil War Monument in Pembroke Center. *Photo by John Proctor.*

for the monument were completed. Only one person, Mrs. Hervey Dyer, refused to serve. The association appointed a committee to investigate the costs and styles of monuments. It was decided that money would be raised by subscription. By 1880, the group had $243 in the fund. This meeting adjourned "subject to call."

Apparently, money was not readily available for such luxuries in this town at that time because it was not until October 1888 that the group met again. Many of the surrounding towns had monuments in place, and Pembroke residents were tired of waiting. By this time, the fund still had only $310. Money was eventually transferred from the Soldiers' Aid Society to the Monument Association, and the Bridgeport Manufacturing Company was commissioned to create a suitable structure at a cost of $950. Suddenly everyone had an opinion that they felt compelled to share. There was much gnashing of teeth and some very vocal arguments, but in spite of it all, on June 12, 1889, the dedication exercises were held. The guest list included state and local dignitaries making lengthy speeches, followed by a poem entitled "Pictures of Pembroke" written and recited by the wife of Dr. O.W. Charles of Bryantville. The ceremonies ended rather abruptly when the visiting guests had to leave to take the trains for home.

When the monument was dedicated, a time capsule was placed either in the monument, as the association notes state, or under the monument, as stated in the official record. In 1991, the Pembroke Town Memorial Committee, led by Bryantville resident Everett Reed, began the task of locating this precious artifact. Unfortunately, it was the official record and not the association notes that were read because, after many months of digging and countless hours of discussion, the capsule was finally found *within* the base of the monument, and a plaque was placed over the hole. The time capsule contained period newspapers, writings, coins and medals. The capsule itself was really a copper box, soldered shut, hopefully to keep out the ravages of time. Sadly, the box was full of water caused by years of condensation and had to be taken to the Northeast Document Center in Andover, Massachusetts, to be restored and preserved. The cost for this process was about $2,000. I wonder what that monument committee would have thought about that!

The monument inscription reads, "Erected by the citizens of Pembroke to commemorate the brave deeds of their local sons in the war for the preservation of the Union 1861–1865."

EPITAPHS AND THE STORIES OF PEMBROKE CITIZENS

One thing just about every New England town has in common is its ancient, historic burying grounds. Frequently, these are located near a church or town green. Sometimes there are small family plots located on what was once a remote part of the family farm or homestead. In the past, like their European counterparts, cemeteries have been cleared from time to time to provide room for newer generations or to return a particularly valuable piece of land to farming use or even to become that twentieth-century innovation known as the housing subdivision. Often, as stones have deteriorated from centuries of weather and other environmental abuse, these pieces of folk art, with their clues to our historic past, are simply discarded without thought. Those of us interested in family and local history understand the significance of such practices and try to make others aware of this irretrievable loss of our heritage.

The epitaphs, carved for all to read, offer a fascinating window into the minds of our ancestors. Epitaphs can be as simple as a name and a birth and/or death date. Others have inscribed on them information about the life or death of an individual. Still others offer fascinating glimpses into the character and even the personality traits of the person resting beneath. And finally, there are those with bits of poetry or religious verse that often indicate the mindset of those left behind to mourn.

A walk through the burying grounds of Pembroke can provide the careful observer with examples of all these types of gravestone prose. I offer the following as examples:

"Erected in memory of the Revd Thomas Smith Pastor of the First Church of Christ in Pembroke. He died July 7: 1788 in his 83rd year." Obviously a man who was proud of his chosen profession.

"Here Lyes Ye Interred Body of the Honourable Isaac Littel Esqir Died February Ye 2D 1758 in Ye 80th Year of His Age." Noting all his titles, this man seems to have been very proud of his life's accomplishments.

"Mrs. Sarah Cushing Ye Vertuous Consort of Captn Nehemiah Cushing Died July Ye 6th 1749 in Har 61st Year Ye Me Behold I Am Mouldering Into Dust/As I Am Now So Sertainly You Must/When This You See Remember Me/For I Am in Eternyte." This woman was probably not a fun-loving soul in life, and the stone carver could have used some spelling lessons.

One gets a totally different opinion of this woman: "Here Lyes The Remains of Mrs. Mary Dunster Relict of the Revd Isiah Dunster of Harwich She Died December 23: 1796 in Har 62 Year She Thro Life With

Equal Ardour Strove/To Taste The Sweets of Friendship And of Love/ With Mutual Warmth Unwelcome Cares Beguiled/And Wept Together And Together Smild."

Finally, this epitaph echoes a story common to so many of our pioneering women: "In Memory of Mrs. Deborah Wife to Mr. Isaac Drake With Her Infant Son On Her Arm Who Died October 23: 1800 Aged 21 Years."

Sabbaday Orchard

Prior to its incorporation as a town in 1712, the lands now known as Pembroke were divided mainly among Duxbury, Marshfield and Scituate.

About 1660, an area of Duxbury known as Mattakeesett was beginning to be settled. The influx of settlers from Europe made it necessary for this westward expansion. These newcomers needed land to farm and raise cattle.

By 1700, the area was dotted with pockets of private dwellings. The farms of Aaron Soule and Josiah Keen were located in East Pembroke. North Pembroke had the Barker and Turner families. The Schoosett area had Holmes and Magoun families. North from Oldham Pond were the Bonneys and Oldhams. Crookertown was being settled by families with the names of Crooker, Ford and Stetson.

Strangely enough, however, there were no public buildings. It was difficult for these various families to socialize. The nearest meetinghouses were in South Marshfield and South Duxbury. For the average family, this meant a twenty-mile journey on Sunday. Because of their devout belief in public worship, it was important for them to establish a meetinghouse in this frontier.

There are two stories relating to the establishment of the Sabbaday Orchard meetings. The first says that the citizens of Mattakeesett petitioned Duxbury for permission to establish a meetinghouse. Permission granted, they sought an appropriate location. The Barker family, who had received a large grant of land about 1628, offered the use of a piece of property located amid a large orchard believed to have been planted by an early Huguenot settler. The earliest meetings were held outdoors, but as colder weather approached, the need for a permanent shelter became apparent. A crude building, not much more than a shed, was erected in the orchard. The shed was still standing until early in this century, although its use was as a storage building.

The second story says that once the residents of Mattakeesett decided to hold worship meetings locally, they started small. They began to meet in the home of Joseph Rogers, who lived among the apple trees of the old Huguenot orchard. This site became known as "Sabbaday Orchard." The local pronunciation "Sabbaday" referred to the fact that it was the site of Sabbath day worship meetings. The actual location of the Rogers house was halfway down the hill on Mountain Avenue, on the left as you head away from Pembroke Center.

By 1706, the group had outgrown the Rogers living room. They began to collect private donations for the purpose of building a meetinghouse. By June 1708, a wood-frame building had been constructed on land near the site of the present First Church in Pembroke. It was used until 1727, when it was replaced by a larger structure.

Whichever version is accurate, two points are the same in each story. The location of the first worship meetings was the old Huguenot orchard, and the desire of the first settlers of Mattakeesett (now Pembroke) to meet and worship regularly was a strong part of their lives.

Part VI

PEMBROKE PLACES

Bay Path

So much of the history of the town of Pembroke is intertwined with the history of its early Native American inhabitants.

One of the main roads from Plymouth to Boston used during the colonial period and known as the Bay Path had its beginnings as the Massachusetts Path. It was the main Indian trail used by the Massachusetts Indians, who controlled this area prior to European settlement. The path ran between Neponset and Mattakeesett (the Indian name for the Pembroke area meaning "place of much fish").

The Pembroke section of this thoroughfare began at the Duxbury line on High Street and continued down High Street to the Herring Run. Here it turned up Center Street to Oldham Street, down Oldham to West Elm Street and on to the Hanover line and beyond.

Local historian Harry Litchfield tells us that although it was generally known that many of the roads in Pembroke started out as Indian trails, it was not known specifically what course many of these roads actually took. About 1905, a Hanson resident, Mercer Tillson, informed a local newspaper that he had been able to trace the course of the long-sought-after Bay Path through Pembroke. Mr. Tillson was a retired foundry worker at the Quincy Iron Works. Retirement had afforded him the time to pursue his interest in surveying. The lucky find of a property deed had given Mr. Tillson the clues necessary for tracing the ancient route through Pembroke.

Bay Path stone marker located on High Street. *Photo by John Proctor.*

Besides the lovely old homes that line this historic thoroughfare, there is another remnant, still visible, left from this period. It is a bridge that crosses the Swamp Brook and is located in a field off West Elm Street. It is believed that the Massachusetts Indians used two paths through this part of Pembroke—the so-called Summer and Winter Paths. The stone bridge is situated on what would have been the Summer Path. The Winter Path ran across the higher ground near where the Pembroke Country Club now stands.

Although it is not known exactly when this stone bridge was built, historic maps and other records, as well as a certain amount of informed speculation, indicate that the bridge was probably used as a foot, horse and cart path prior to 1682. It remained an important link in the local transportation network until about 1830. At this time, old maps of Pembroke indicate that the course of West Elm Street was altered and straightened to its present location and that the original path and the old stone bridge fell out of service.

Pembroke's portion of the Bay Path has withstood centuries of development and alteration. Through it all, however, it remains a testament to Pembroke's fortunate location and abundant natural resources. We can only hope that this pastoral piece of pre-colonial and colonial history will survive for centuries to come.

THE BRICK KILN SHIPYARD

During the heyday of shipbuilding on the North River (the mid-nineteenth century), there were a total of fifteen shipyards along its banks. Several of these yards were located in Pembroke. These were the Turner Yard, Seabury's Point and the Job's Landing and Brick Kiln Shipyards. Shipbuilding on the North River actually spanned three centuries, from the late 1660s with the Turner and Smith families until the launching of the last ship built on the river, the *Helen M. Foster*, in 1871.

Perhaps the busiest and most famous of all the Pembroke shipyards was the Brick Kiln Yard. It is unclear exactly when shipbuilding began at this site because this part of Pembroke was part of other towns until 1712, when Pembroke was incorporated. Although it is widely believed that the Brick Kiln Yard was flourishing by the year 1730, the first actual record we have is for that year, when Captain Benjamin Turner moved to Pembroke and built at the Brick Kiln Yard. Captain Ichabod Thomas, who learned his trade from Captain Turner, built at the Brick Kiln from 1764 to 1788.

L. Vernon Briggs, in his book *History of Shipbuilding on the North River*, states, "At no [other] yard on the North River were such a number of famous ships built." One of the most famous ships believed to have been built here was

Site of the Brick Kiln Shipyard on the North River. *From the collection of Ed Leadbetter.*

the *Beaver*, one of the tea party ships of Boston Harbor from which tea was thrown overboard by angry colonists in 1773.

Another Brick Kiln ship, the *Somerset*, carried papers sent by Benjamin Franklin (who was in Europe at the time) to the Continental Congress in Philadelphia announcing a treaty with France made during the American Revolution.

The *Bedford*, built by Ichabod Thomas at Brick Kiln, was the first vessel to carry the American Stars and Stripes into a British port in 1782.

The *Maria*, built in 1782, was in active service longer than any other ship built on the North River. It sailed for over ninety years and is the ship immortalized by Everett Reed on the seal of the town of Pembroke.

Other ships built at the Brick Kiln with names like *Harmony*, *Leo* and *Falkland*, as well as many others, sailed the world and kept their owners, as well as their ports of call, well supplied with goods from far-off, exotic locations.

After Captain Thomas, the families of Lewis, Briggs, Sampson, Rogers, Hatch and Magoun all built ships at the Brick Kiln. In 1841, the Honorable John Quincy Adams, then in Congress, came to visit the towns of Hanover, Scituate, Pembroke and Marshfield at the invitation of the North River shipbuilders. He came on a fact-finding mission to collect data that might help him in his efforts to obtain an appropriate sum of money from Congress to dredge a new, wider mouth on the North River by cutting through a sandbar or through the beach. Unfortunately, his efforts failed, and as a result, with the demand for larger ships and the dwindling supply of lumber at the Brick Kiln site, by 1848–50, shipbuilding at the Brick Kiln Ship Yard had ended.

BURTON HOMESTEAD

According to the late town historian Harry Litchfield, in 1729/30, Thomas Burton—the son of Stephen Burton, a prominent citizen of Rhode Island, and Elizabeth Winslow, the only daughter of Governor Josiah Winslow of Marshfield—purchased a piece of land in Pembroke and built his home. He married Alice Wadsworth of Duxbury. A well-educated man, he became the second schoolmaster of Pembroke. In this home, Thomas and Alice Burton raised three daughters, having lost one in childhood.

In 1766, Thomas and Alice's youngest daughter, Elizabeth, or "Mistress Betty Burton," as she was known, married Daniel Bonney, and they purchased a half interest in the family homestead. Elizabeth and Daniel had no children, so when she died in 1807, Daniel sold the home the next year to Elisha Keen Josselyn, an anchor smith from Pembroke.

The present house was built by Elisha Keen Josselyn, and the original building became an ell. Historian Litchfield goes on to tell us that early in the nineteenth century, "the ancient Burton house was detached from that of Mr. Josselyn's construction and moved to the opposite side of the street." Part of the building was kept by Mr. Josselyn as a general store, from which, we are told by Litchfield, "the Josselyns dispensed a goodly measure of strong drink to their customers."

Elisha Josselyn died in 1857, his widow died in 1863 and the home passed to their son James Riley Josselyn. In 1878, a room was rented from J. Riley in the homestead for use as Pembroke's first free public library, where it remained for the next twelve years. An increase in the rent of the room to ten dollars per year caused the library to be moved to the Ladies Sewing Circle building, where it remained until 1958.

In a style of writing that only Harry Litchfield could evoke, he writes, "The last…of the Burtons sleep…in Pembroke Burying Ground…the ancient dwelling is instinct with memory of them." Isn't this true of most of the homes in Pembroke?

Burton Homestead at the corner of Center Street and Mattakeesett Street. *Pembroke Historical Society.*

That home, which stands at the corner of Center and Mattakeesett Streets, is known historically as the Burton Homestead. A few years ago, when threatened with being torn down and replaced with a modern structure, residents of Pembroke expressed their dismay, and the plans for the building were changed. A modified Burton Homestead became the Rockland Trust Bank, and a little piece of Pembroke history was preserved.

THE FIRST PARISH SEWING CIRCLE

It is a small building in the center of Pembroke that is often overlooked as we hurry by on our way to somewhere else. It sits directly across the street from the First Church. The "First Parish Sewing Circle" represents one of the oldest social gatherings in Pembroke, as it was started in 1845 by a group of First Parish women as an aid to the church and any other worthwhile charitable organization in town.

Sewing Circle building, circa 1912. *Pembroke Historical Society.*

This group had been meeting unofficially for social and charitable purposes for some years before it gained official status. On Tuesday, November 4, 1845, after reading a posted notice the previous Sunday at First Church, a group of women met at the Pembroke Town Hall to form the Pembroke Ladies Sewing Circle. This first meeting wrote, "Acknowledging the kindly influence of our former Society—hoping that while our hands are gathering the gold that perisheth, our hearts may be laying up treasure neither moth nor rust doth corrupt—We do invite all who feel an interest in the support of Christianity, in feeding the hungry [and] clothing the naked, to meet with us on Wednesday at one o'clock with willing hearts and ready hands for the above named purpose."

At this meeting, the following officers were elected: Mrs. Mary C. Barker, moderator; Mrs. Caroline Collamore, president; Mrs. Mary S. Hatch, vice-president; and Miss Martha J. Allen, secretary and treasurer. The following bylaws were also drawn up:

> *1. That we will meet on each alternate Wednesday at one o'clock and work until 8. If not convenient to attend each meeting we will pay a fine of 6-¼ cents for each omission. If not pleasant on Wednesday, we will meet on the next fair day.*
>
> *2. Any person interested in promoting the objects of our society, and not feeling convenient to attend our meetings, may become an honorary member with right to vote and not subject to fine by paying $1.00 per year.*

From left to right: Abbie Oldham, Phoebe Baker, Mrs. Miller, Carrie Thayer, Nellie Bates, Alice Litchfield and Annie Anderson. Standing on the stairs are Deborah Ramsdell, Eva Crne, Dorothea Ford, Besse Porter and Mary Addie Oldham. *First Church in Pembroke.*

> *3. Any person not wishing to become a member, yet disposed to cultivate a friendly and social feeling and help a good work, we would cordially invite to meet with us when they feel disposed.*

Over the next few years, the meetings were apparently held at various homes.

In 1851, it was decided that a fair should be held in October to pay for the repair of the Central Burying Ground in Pembroke. Abigail Standish Josselyn, then president of the society, was largely responsible for erecting the iron and stone fence around the cemetery. At this time, a new constitution was adopted by the Sewing Society. It contained eleven articles. Article I stated that the official name of the society would be the "Sewing Circle of the First Parish in Pembroke." The purpose of the society would be to "assist according to its means the religious society in said Parish and the Sabbath School connected therewith."

Perhaps because of the success of the fair and the encouragement of the town, it was decided at a meeting in 1857 that a meeting and social gathering place of their own should be built. A committee consisting of Seth and Thomas Whitman and John Oldham was asked to get cost

Sewing Circle ladies, circa 1943. *First Church in Pembroke.*

estimates. It was eventually voted to build a structure "30 feet in length and 20 feet wide." The cost of the building was $483.92. A lease was signed by Nathaniel Smith to the Ladies Sewing Society giving them a certain piece of land for their building.

Eventually, land turned over to the society by Susan Smith and Almire Bonney made up the entire parcel of land now owned by the Sewing Circle. In 1874, the society voted that the building should be turned over to the First Church in Pembroke should the Sewing Society ever be dissolved. Since that time, the ranks of the little social and charitable group swelled and diminished many times.

On November 6, 1988, these words were spoken: "I think we should still get together socially twice a year—at Christmas and once in the spring." Nods of agreement came from the seven members present. "Now, let's have lunch." And with those words, the last business meeting of the oldest social/civic/religious organization in the town of Pembroke, which had begun with a blessing by the Reverend David L. Clarke, pastor of the First Church in Pembroke, came to an inauspicious end. After 148 years of active participation for the benefit of the members of the First Church and the community as a whole, the First Parish Sewing Circle marked the end of an era. In attendance were circle president Joan Dunn, Taimi Maki, Constance Shepherd, Helen Wyman, Germaine Corbett, Eleanor

Scheumann and Joan D'Alessandro. Seven more members—Martina Campbell, Jo Cande, Frances Fuller, Mary Ford, Emma Hollows, Louise Howe and Barbara Bucknam—were unable to attend. The demands of work, failing health and the pain of seeing the end of a group some had seen their mothers and grandmothers attend proved too much for a few. Several active, longtime members had passed away since their last Christmas meeting. But looking around at the group assembled, you felt that they were all there—at least in the hearts and memories of those left behind.

So today, although the formal First Parish Sewing Circle has passed into history, the legacy of its good and charitable work remains. The tiny building is run by the First Church as a thrift shop.

THE GAR HALL

After the conclusion of the Civil War, veterans groups like the GAR (Grand Army of the Republic) began to spring up throughout the northern states. Returning veterans needed jobs; President Lincoln had promised care for the veterans and their widows and children. However, the government was not sure how to go about what seemed like a daunting task, and the veterans themselves were feeling the need to continue the bonds formed soldier to soldier during the war.

The first formal group honoring the Civil War veterans of the army, navy and marines was formed in Decatur, Illinois, by Benjamin F. Stephenson in 1866. It was open to all veterans who had been honorably discharged and had served between April 12, 1861, and April 9, 1865.

As a political force to be reckoned with, the organization founded soldiers' homes and promoted pension legislation.

Pembroke's veterans began meeting on a regular basis in the year 1869. These first meetings were held at Mechanics Hall on High Street (now the High Street fire station). At that time, there were eleven charter members.

It was decided that this newly chartered Post 111 should have a name. Bailey Damon suggested that it be named after Joseph E. Simmons, a Pembroke resident who had been killed at the Battle of Second Manassas (Bull Run) in Northern Virginia. Bailey had been seriously wounded in the same battle. From 1881 to 1887, Post 111 met at East Pembroke. After that, it began meeting at the town hall.

GAR Hall, Pembroke Center, now the Pembroke Police Boys' Club. *Pembroke Historical Society.*

There had been in existence a patriotic group of Pembroke women known as the Grand Army Sewing Circle. In 1891, this group became known as the Jos. E. Simmons Women's Relief Corps. They had been meeting first at the town hall and later over Lewis Howe's store. The room was small and "inconvenient" for their work. The ladies then decided it was time to consider building a hall for themselves and their "comrades" in the GAR. After conferring with the men's group, it was decided that the project of building a suitable meeting place would have to fall on the women, as none of the men wanted to assume the responsibility. The men would, however, "render all the assistance they could." By 1896, the new hall was ready. It was dedicated in September of that year, and the women of the WRC invited their GAR comrades to share the hall with them.

Many of the veterans have familiar Pembroke names like Presby, Poole, Magoun, Sampson, Farnsworth, Phillips, Collamore, Damon, Gaskins, Halliday, Ford, Hatch, Drake, Mann, Tappan and Morton.

You have probably passed by this little piece of patriotic history hundreds of times. It is currently the Pembroke Police Boys' Club located next to the senior center. It has also served as a meeting place for Pembroke's Sons of Union Veterans and the VFW (Veterans of Foreign Wars).

HOSEA'S

If you lived in Pembroke in the 1930s right through 2007, there is a good chance you knew about Hosea's Restaurant/Café on Mattakeesett Street at Furnace Pond. What began as a roadside stand selling hot dogs, sodas, ice cream and other snack foods became a local "watering hole," according to Ed Quill in *Pembroke 2000* before it closed in 2007 to be reborn as the Lucky Dawg.

Hosea Delano Benson was born in Kingston, Massachusetts, on December 28, 1900. He was one of two children born to Edmund and Sylvia (Hernandez) Benson. His father listed his occupation as foreman in a shoe factory. The family lived in Middleborough and Hanson during Hosea's formative years. About 1920, Hosea Benson started his working career as a conductor on the electric railway.

Hosea began a life as a victualer in 1928, when he began working at the Brown Betty, a popular Dixieland music and dance spot located at the

Benson's Café. *Pembroke Historical Society.*

Hosea Benson, circa 1945. *Pembroke Historical Society.*

corner of Mattakeesett and Wampatuck Streets. Soon, Hosea opened a small "Brown Betty Annex" just down the road from the original building where snack-type food was sold to bathers from the beach, bathhouse and boat rental spot newly created nearby.

In 1933, Hosea opened his new place, named Hosea's, across the street on Furnace Pond. In the 1940s, he expanded the snack stand to include a bar and lunch spot and eventually turned it into a full restaurant.

According to Ed Quill, Hosea put together a street fair every year on Mattakeesett Street, giving away hot dogs, soda and popcorn to the local children. In the evening, there were fireworks.

About 1964, Hosea and his wife, Mary, gave up their careers as victualers. Hosea died in 1980 and Mary in 1987. The establishment was sold but kept the same name; in the 1990s, the bar side was badly damaged by a fire and had to be closed while renovations occurred.

Today, Hosea's has been transformed into the Lucky Dawg Tavern and Grille, a pub fare–style family restaurant that also serves take-out ice cream. It almost sounds like everything old is new again!

THE KING'S HIGHWAY

For over two hundred years, the stretch of today's Route 53 that ran through Pembroke was part of a stagecoach route that ran from Boston to Plymouth. Although originally used by the mail coaches of the day, as the residents of the area began to move out of the cramped cities and into the more rural areas more and more, the stagecoaches were used by passengers traveling from one city to another. In the years prior to the American Revolution, this route was known, not surprisingly, as the King's Highway.

Because the early roads were little more than dirt paths through the wilderness, stagecoach travel was slow and difficult. Frequent stops had to be made, not only as part of mail and passenger delivery, but also to care for the horses and make repairs to the coaches. Each stagecoach line had depots or stopping places along the route and tried to maintain a fairly regular schedule. This allowed for the pickup of new passengers, as well as an opportunity for weary travelers to get exercise, food and the opportunity for rest, should they be going a long distance.

These depots soon expanded their services and became inns, catering to the needs of these travelers. One such spot, the King's Highway Inn, is still located at its original spot on Route 53. The inn was built on a tract of land given to Francis Barker by his father, Robert Baker, one of the first settlers of Pembroke. It is believed to have been built about 1660 because, during one of the inn's restorations, a hammered copper horseshoe-shaped plate

King's Highway Inn. *Pembroke Historical Society.*

King's Highway Inn advertisement. *From the collection of Ed Leadbetter.*

bearing that date was uncovered. It had been built into the center chimney. In 1713, Francis Barker gave the house to his daughter Ruth, who had married Cornelius Briggs. In these early years, the inn was used as a tavern. In 1761, it was purchased by Dr. Jeremiah Hall, Pembroke's first physician. Dr. Hall served as a surgeon in the French and Indian War and the Revolutionary War. He was also one of the Pembroke citizens who signed the Pembroke Resolves. The inn was later owned by Horace Collamore, who had married Laurentia, the granddaughter of Dr. Hall. They ran a country store and post office in the old inn. Mr. Collamore was a representative and senator in the general court of Massachusetts. He also financed many shipbuilding projects, including the *Mattakees*, the only steamboat ever built on the North River.

The King's Highway Inn is considered one of the oldest structures in Pembroke. Those who have owned the house have kept many of the original details, including several early wooden door latches, crude leather strap "H" hinges, pegged and joined oak beams, some early windows and glass and "King's Ransom" floorboards. Over the years, in addition to being used off and on as an inn, the rear addition was used in 1867 by the F.P. Arnold Company for the manufacturing of shoes. This business prospered to the point where eventually it was moved nearby and employed over one hundred men, using the most modern shoe-making machinery. The building has also been a restaurant, the barn was a hobby shop and the structure is currently partly a private home and partly an apartment dwelling.

MECHANICS HALL

The year was 1906 when the *Bryantville News* reported that much interest was being stirred up on High Street near the Duxbury line. The old Mechanics Hall (now the High Street Fire Station) was being remodeled and would soon serve once again as a place for dancing and entertainment.

The hall had been a landmark of sorts for at least two generations. The building had been moved to its present location in 1865 by Hiram Randall and William Stetson from neighboring Hanover, where it had been used as a recruiting station and site for military drills. Once moved to Pembroke, it was used as an academy. About a year after it was moved, Mr. Randall bought out Mr. Stetson, and a third story was added. The top floor served as a dance hall, the second floor was used as a carriage shop and the first floor became a wheelwright shop.

For twenty or more years, Mechanics Hall was the dancing center for the area. Couples from Hanson, Kingston, Rockland, Hanover and elsewhere came to dance all night and drive home in the morning light. Times, however, changed, and the interest in "dancing 'til dawn" waned. By the end of the last century, the hall was being used for various lodge meetings and became the headquarters for Pembroke's temperance union. In 1900, the building, having been sadly neglected, was pronounced unsafe.

Mechanics Hall stood empty for a number of years until a group of interested and concerned High Street–area residents formed the "High Street Hall Association." Shares were sold for five dollars each until enough money was raised to buy the old building, repair it and put on an addition at the rear for a stage. Two years later, a Grand Masquerade Ball ushered in a new beginning for the old hall. Also at that time, the High Street area firemen held their first meeting, and in 1912, they bought the hall.

The early fire brigade had two horse-drawn chemical wagons that were not kept in the firemen's building but rather in neighborhood barns until much later, when two bays were added for them.

Keeping up the $49.80-a-year mortgage payments was not easy for this small, independent fire brigade. "Firemen's Hall," as it had become known, was kept alive by numerous strawberry festivals, turkey shoots, dances,

Mechanics Hall, now the High Street Fire Station. *Photo by John Proctor.*

suppers and concerts. At one point, with the possibility of immediate closing looming near, the residents of the High Street area sent donations of $0.50 to $2.00 to keep the station open.

Eventually, two more fire companies were added to Pembroke's Fire Department. Each company had fifteen call firemen. The Center Street Station had twenty full-time firemen, a chief and a secretary.

OLDHAM FARM

Oldham Street is often used by Pembroke residents as an alternate route to Hanover or Hanson. Its name comes from the Oldham family—early settlers and prominent residents of our town—who lived on the shores of Oldham Pond for many generations.

Thomas Oldham, son of the Thomas Oldham who was an early settler of Scituate, purchased from Jeremiah, "Indian of Mattakeesett, and Abigail, his wife or squa," a tract of land consisting of about one hundred acres on

Oldham Farm on Oldham Street. *Photo by John Proctor.*

the north shore of what was then known as Monument (now Oldham) Pond. He paid fourteen pounds silver for the land in 1693. The land was one-tenth of the "Thousand Acres"—land set aside in 1662 by Josiah Wampatuck, Sachem of the Massachusetts Indians, for himself and his heirs. Mattakeesett was the name given by the Native Americans to the land that eventually became Pembroke.

It appears from the records that Thomas never settled on the property. In 1695, he gave half of his land "at Mattakeesett" to his brother Isaac Oldham, who, it is believed, built a dwelling and soon after married Hannah Keen of Duxbury. Pembroke records indicate the couple had three children.

Isaac worked the farm for forty years, until his death in 1736. Isaac's son Isaac inherited the homestead and lived in his father's house with his wife, Mary (Stetson), and their four children until he died in 1796. Mary died in 1808. By this time, the original dwelling was in a very poor state of repair, and it was left to David Oldham Jr., the great-grandson of pioneer Isaac, to tear down the original dwelling and rebuild on the family's ancestral Pembroke land when he inherited it in 1804.

David Oldham, Esquire
1776 - 1857

David Oldham. *Pembroke Historical Society.*

David Oldham, Esquire, was a man of prominence in Pembroke. He was a member of the board of selectmen for eighteen years. He also served as town moderator and held many offices as a member of the First Parish Church in Pembroke. He was married to Deborah Barker, a descendant of the first Pembroke settler, Robert Barker. David and Deborah raised eight children in the home. David Oldham died in Pembroke in 1857. His cause of death was listed as "debility." Deborah died in

Camp Pembroke girls' camp. *From the collection of Ed Leadbetter.*

1861 of "influenza." After their deaths, the Oldham farm passed out of the family.

More recently, the property has been used by Catholic charities as a boys' summer camp and is currently known as Camp Pembroke, a summer camp for girls of the Jewish faith. This seems a fitting use for a property that has seen the growth and development of so many generations of Pembroke families with children.

THE PEMBROKE ALMS HOUSE

Have you ever said to your children or your spouse, "At this rate, we'll be in the poorhouse by the end of the year," referring to some spending excess or lack of good judgment in the banking area?

Today, when we use these words, most of the time we are joking. But to our great-grandfathers, this threat was very real and only as remote a possibility as a bad year for crops or an illness that prevented the family breadwinner from working.

Today, the idea of the town poor farm calls to mind some scene out of a Charles Dickens novel where a number of pathetically undernourished individuals are forced to perform work, akin to slave labor, by a cruel overseer with a whip.

The first records concerning the treatment of the poor in Pembroke begin in the year 1813. These books indicate that a man was appointed by the selectmen to be the overseer of the poor. He was responsible for seeing that housing arrangements were made for the less fortunate.

Usually, various townspeople who had room would agree to take the poor into their homes for a period of time and would accept a small payment for their service, or they would take payment in the form of work by the person, if he were able.

Sometimes, a poor, young person was "indentured" or "bound out" to a member of the community who was well established. The young person would work for a specified period of time and often learn a trade. This system was in effect until 1823, when it was decided that a new method of dealing with the problem of the poor was needed.

Eventually, almost every town instituted the idea of a poor farm, or almshouse, as they were sometimes called. Pembroke's was located on Mattakeesett Street across from the ballfields. The building still remains and has been turned into an apartment house. It was originally the Parris farm and was purchased in 1823 for less than $3,500 including stock, utensils and so forth. A tract of land opposite, on the Darling farm, was also purchased for $700.

A board of twelve overseers was elected to make the poorhouse a going concern. Isaac Stetson and his wife were chosen as overseers of the poorhouse for a fee of $200 for a year of service. They were expected to keep the cost of running the farm to a minimum. Dr. Anthony Collamore was to be the physician and surgeon to the poor for a fee of $15 per year.

The board of overseers set out strict and specific rules that were to be observed within the poorhouse in Pembroke:

> *The Overseer of the Poor House shall observe impartiality to all as far as their bodily condition and decency of conduct will permit.*
>
> *The Overseer shall see that good order is preserved throughout the House and the Poor are to observe all his orders and commands.*
>
> *He is to enjoin the necessity of cleanliness upon each member of the family.*
>
> *Breakfast shall consist of rye coffee sweetened with molasses, or of chocolate or shelly with molasses, sweet bread occasionally, or if with chocolate, brown bread crumbed therein, or bread and milk, or porridge; the women to have tea with molasses.*

The dinner shall be Indian pudding or rice pudding with molasses sauce one or two days each week and meat or fish of some kind all other days mainly served as stews or soups.

The supper shall consist of bread and milk, milk porridge or gruel sweetened with molasses, domestic coffee, chocolate broth or hasty pudding. Tea is served to the whole family only once a week with bread and butter.

Sunday meals should be breakfast and late dinner with tea for all who prefer it.

The Overseer is to be at the table for all meals to see that no one wastes food or leaves any on their plates

The Overseer can place people at different tables, but all are to be served the same food unless they are ill.

No liquor or wine is allowed except under the direction of the physician.

The members of the House cannot leave the premises except with the permission of the Overseer. They are to be in bed by 8 p.m. during the winter months and 9 p.m. during the summer months. No lights are allowed without the permission of the Overseer.

By 1825, it had become clear that a new addition to the poorhouse system was necessary. It was called the "House of Industry." The rules and regulations that follow give us a good idea of the purpose of this new institution:

It is expedient that a place of confinement be provided at the [Poor] *House for the refractory and disobedient, who may be restrained when the good order of the House requires it.*

Each person committed to the House be placed under the direction of the Overseer, whose reasonable commands he shall obey and whose continuance in said House shall depend on his conduct while in it.

Each person committed to the House, during good behavior, shall be comfortable, fed, clothed and lodged, and employed, if able, under the direction of the Overseer.

No ardent spirits shall be given to the inmate except under the direction of the physician.

For the encouragement of sobriety, good conduct and industry, the Overseers of the House shall keep and account of extra labors of those who pay more than their expenses, so they may be considered by the Board for special benefit.

That those persons described by the act for whom the House of Industry is provided, be sent there without any distinction or partiality, that pauperism may be prevented.

The institution seems to have worked quite well. By 1829, the overseers reported that this system "was the most humane and economical that could be adopted." While the overseers realized that the poorhouse concept was distasteful to some, they believed there were those who were grateful for the basic necessities of life the house provided, which they would otherwise not have available to them.

Prior to the year 1832, no provision was made for the "demented," so in that year, the overseers went to the town meeting to "know the mind of the town; whether a House shall be built for the purpose of confining the refractory, mad or idle persons at the Poor House."

In November 1832, a committee was chosen for the purpose of erecting a building at the poorhouse for those persons who otherwise neglected and refused to provide for their families. Specifications were clearly set out, and two men were chosen to superintend the building.

Over the next decade, both white and Indian men, women and children were taken care of at the poorhouse. The farm provided for the needs of the residents, and surpluses were sold. The women took care of the housework, and the men went to work for the town, building roads and bridges.

There were two other types of individuals who could be admitted to the poorhouse family. The first were the federal pensioners who received a regular income from former war service. The second type was the state

Pembroke Alms House on Mattakeesett Street. *Pembroke Historical Society.*

pauper who was state supported until state wardship was abolished in 1869. The Native Americans fell into this latter group.

The Pembroke poorhouse was in operation until 1947, when it was sold by the town. It seems apparent that the roots of today's homeless shelters can be traced back to this vanished institution.

Although the rules were strict and the lifestyle severe, each member of the family was provided with food and a roof over their head, two basics of life that are not necessarily provided to all today.

THE PEMBROKE HISTORICAL SOCIETY

Beginning in the latter half of the last century, local residents of many towns throughout America, and especially in New England, had the foresight to begin to preserve records and mementos of the past. You can visit these halls of memories (usually by appointment, although many have regular hours), and the experience is a fun and fascinating look at the way we were.

Pembroke Historical Society Museum on Center Street. *Pembroke Historical Society.*

I am speaking about local historical societies, and while, over the years, they seem to have earned a reputation for being stuffy and dull, they are usually merely dusty and full of wonderful surprises—a collective grandma's attic of amazing glimpses into the past.

The Pembroke Historical Society Museum, located at 116 Center Street, was originally built in 1847 and served as the Bryantville School. It was built on School Street and housed all eight grades in one room. In 1911, a newer two-room school was built, and the building was sold to Pearly Reed for $250. It was moved to Center Street, where the building was used by Mr. Reed and, later, Marcus Urann in the cranberry business. It was Mr. Urann's friendship with George Edward Lewis, one of the founders of the historical society, that led him to eventually donate the building to the society.

The Pembroke Historical Society was organized in 1950. Records of the first meeting indicate that it was thought that once the new society was formed, residents of Pembroke would make donations of historical data, furniture and other items so that a regular "historic room" could be maintained. By the third meeting of the society, held in June 1950, there were over one hundred charter members. The first honorary membership was bestowed on Harry W. Litchfield, author of *Ancient Landmarks of Pembroke*, a book that is still available today from the historical society.

In 1968, the former Cedar Swamp School located on West Elm Street was moved to its present location as a meeting hall attached to the rear of the museum to help with the expanding needs of the society.

The residents of our town, both past and present, have been very generous with their memories, time and talents. In 1988, the museum building was dedicated to the memory of the late Bonney Sherman, curator of the historical society for twenty years.

Each spring, society members, volunteers and parents host the annual "Old Pembroke Days Children's Program" for the town's fifth-grade students. For three days, the society's buildings ring with the footsteps of busy children learning about life in colonial Pembroke. The society also runs the "Grand Old Fashioned Fish Fry" each year.

In May 2000, as the world celebrated a new millennium, the Pembroke Historical Society celebrated its fiftieth anniversary under the capable leadership of Brooks Kelly. Up until this time, the society concentrated on Pembroke history from the seventeenth, eighteenth and nineteenth centuries. It now has expanded its focus to consider the twentieth century as history as well.

PEMBROKE'S TOWN FORESTS AND PUBLIC LANDS

The year was 1924. The annual meeting of the Town of Pembroke voted to join a growing movement of other Massachusetts cities and towns in setting aside tracts of land for public recreational use. Pembroke residents voted to set aside a portion of the former town farm (poorhouse) on Mattakeesett Street as a town forest. This action provided a protected area in which nature, with the careful help and planning of man, could develop into a "sanctuary of green growth" that would be preserved for future generations. In addition to the natural stand of trees, five thousand pine trees, a gift from the Massachusetts Forestry Association, were planted along the forest's eastern ridge. At this time, the Town Forest Committee included J.J. Shepherd, E.P. Litchfield, W.A. Key and Stanley B. Hall. In 1929, to honor the public service of its late selectman J.J. Shepherd, the town voted to name the forest the J.J. Shepherd Memorial Town Forest.

Mr. Shepherd was an ardent supporter of conservation and the town forest law. Such supporters believed that "whenever a town has applied good business methods to land management, the Town has in its Forest, an investment which will pay dividends in the sale of forest products, water protection, recreation, wild life propagation, education, and beautification

J.J. Shepherd Memorial Town Forest. *Photo by John Proctor.*

of the town." The open fields soon became a favorite gathering place for athletic contests and other outdoor recreational activities.

Explanatory signs crafted by pupils of Pembroke's industrial arts course at the entrance to the forest served to remind residents of the importance of the town forest as one of the town's most prized possessions. The Massachusetts Forest and Park Association, in its 1956 progress report of town forests in Massachusetts, wrote:

> *One of the more outstanding town forests in Massachusetts which has sold itself to local residents is the 100 acre J.J. Shepherd Memorial Town Forest in Pembroke. It has become a community center for many types of family activities. A portion of the area has been left to open fields. Here a Little League baseball field has been developed. On another portion of the field the local veterans organizations hold their local carnivals and rodeos. The forest provides cool pine groves for picnics and nature walks. Youth groups have their cook-outs and overnight camps there…Although no other town in Massachusetts has developed their town forest to the extent that Pembroke has, many have served in other ways to meet public needs.*

Once again, Pembroke was on the cutting edge of an important issue of the day.

Soon, the Town Forest Committee was informed by Selectman Arthur B. Donnell that two parcels of land that had been taken by the town due to unpaid taxes were also available. So pleased were the citizens of Pembroke about their first town forest that they voted to set aside the over-fifty-acre parcel as a new town forest. The land ran along School Street and bordered today's Pembroke Community Middle School.

According to Mel B. Shepherd, "The name for this forest, The Veteran's Commemorative Town Forest, was selected by the Town Forest Committee, and was voted on by the town in 1969. The word 'commemorative' was chosen because it included living veterans as well as those who had given their lives in service of our country."

In 1956, a twenty-nine-plus-acre parcel of land on Birch Street was taken by tax title. It consisted of cut-over forest. Today, the Birch Street Playground is a part of this parcel.

The residents of Pembroke hoped that eventually all Pembroke residents would live within easy walking distance of a town forest area.

In 1976, the Pembroke Conservation Commission acquired a piece of land made up of about one hundred acres in and around the Great Cedar Swamp. Originally owned by Joshua Cushing, the land was sold to Isaac

Above, left: Veterans' Commemorative Town Forest. *Photo by John Proctor.*

Above, right: Bicentennial Nature Trail, off Littles Avenue. *Photo by John Proctor.*

Right: Tubb's Meadow Brook Preserve. *Photo by John Proctor.*

Little around 1700 and is still known historically today as the Littles' Estate. It remained in the Little family until 1953, when it was sold to Phillip Shannon, and in 1973 it was purchased by the Town of Pembroke.

In 1976, the conservation commission, with a matching grant from the Massachusetts Bicentennial Commission, created a nature trail that starts at the end of Littles Avenue and follows an old wagon road through upland forest and wetlands adjacent to the Great Cedar Swamp.

Over the years, town meeting has added such public land areas as the Willow Brook Nature Preserve and Tubb's Meadow Brook Nature Preserve, all in keeping with the spirit of the original concept of the Pembroke Town Forest Committee.

Pembroke's Town Common and the Pound

Most New England towns, especially those whose roots are firmly established in an agricultural economy, had some tract of land near the town center called the town common. The name comes from the fact that the land was under the jurisdiction of the town and therefore belonged to all the residents in common. Every acre of a family's property was precious to them and usually used for the raising of food, especially corn and hay for winter use. Cattle usually ran at large and foraged for themselves from early spring until late autumn. The common land provided the farmers a place to graze their animals without using up valuable cultivated acreage.

Pembroke's common is first mentioned in town records in 1712 when, on October 20 of that year, the town "granted liberty to all persons belonging to Pembroke to build stables on the Common." Cattle, sheep, swine and horses were allowed to run at large on the common. The swine must be "ringd and Yoakd according to the Province Law," and the ears of all animals must be slit in a pattern forming the owner's private device or earmark (in other words, an early form of the American western custom of branding).

It is hard to know exactly what the boundaries of the common were. Records of 1713 mention that the common was located near the meetinghouse (today called the First Church) and was probably bounded by the cemetery gate and the area around Littles Avenue down Center Street past the present town hall. We do have records that indicate that in 1730 the town received in an exchange a lot of land from Abraham Pearce that became part of the common and later was mostly included as part of the cemetery.

The Pembroke Town Pound in Pembroke Center. *Pembroke Historical Society.*

Quite naturally, the common became an intersecting point for early highways. It is possible to trace the early roads now intersecting the area as direct routes to the homes of the early settlers of Pembroke who would come to check on their livestock. In January 1716, the town voted that "a school be kept half a year annually in ye middle of said town by ye meeting house." The site very likely was where the present Pembroke Historical Society Museum is today. It must have been quite distracting, especially in the warmer months, to attend school and try to pay attention to a teacher over the bleating of sheep and the lowing of cattle.

Besides the meetinghouse and the school, there was built a wooden pound. The location of this structure is not exactly known. The pound served as a detention facility for stray animals and other four-legged invaders of the otherwise undisturbed animal population. The first mention of the present pound (located in front of the town hall) is in March 1824, when the town voted to build a new stone pound with walls five and a half feet high, three feet thick at the bottom and one foot at the top with a pine cap eight inches thick. The gate was to be made of white oak. The new pound was to be the same size as the old one in the

Close-up of Pembroke Pound sign. *Photo by John Proctor.*

clear. This turned out to be twenty feet on all sides. It was also to be near the site of the old pound. Today, according to an article in the March 1974 *Yankee* magazine, although almost every town had one, there are only about twelve town pounds left in existence, including our own. Next time you round the corner by the town hall, take a look at this almost extinct piece of New England Americana.

THE STORES OF NORTH PEMBROKE

What did our Pembroke ancestors ever do without shopping malls and Internet shopping? Here is a little peek.

The spirit of entrepreneurial endeavor that began to sweep America after the Revolutionary War was strongly evidenced in New England. Pembroke was no exception.

Perhaps because of its proximity to the North River and the wealthy shipbuilding families, the area of North Pembroke became a haven for those in the area who wished to spend their hard-earned money or credit on store-bought and/or manufactured items. In addition, there were those necessities that had to be purchased by the average citizen, such as shoes, harnesses for horses, metalware and the like.

One such store, known to the locals as the "Old Brick Store," was run by Bailey Hall, a hatter by trade and son of Dr. Jeremiah Hall, around 1826.

The building itself was constructed from bricks made at the "old clay pit place" on Pleasant Street. The store was kept for many years by Horace Collamore, who was also the postmaster.

A typical American general store, everything you could possibly think of was kept at the Old Brick Store. It is said that the candy case was one of the most well stocked in both quantity and variety of any store in the area. You could also purchase cotton cloth at eleven to fifteen cents a yard. Linen, silk handkerchiefs, ladies' kid gloves, thread and hairbrushes were part of the regular stock. Also, molasses at thirty cents a gallon, coffee, butter, brown sugar, Holland Gin and N.E. Rum could be purchased. Eventually, the Old Brick Store went out of business.

For a few years, another store run by Allen Blackman took its place, but it, too, was later moved to a different location and used as a private residence.

Another well-known store in the North Pembroke area was the Simmons Store, built in 1873. The store was built with a large dance floor upstairs. There was a store located at the West Box Factory that was kept by Calvin Shepherd. This store was also built around 1830, as was a grocery store run by Captain Morton on or near the corner of Pleasant and Washington Streets.

Simmons Store on Washington Street in North Pembroke. *Pembroke Historical Society.*

Another local entrepreneur was Aunt Prussy Ford, a tailoress who went from house to house tailoring for twenty-five cents per day. Unfortunately, her fitting ability sometimes left a bit to be desired, and it was said that if you saw someone with rather ill-fitting clothes, they were probably the work of dear old Aunt Prussy.

There were also a number of small stores located on Brick Kiln Lane that provided the shipbuilders of Pembroke with their needed supplies.

So you see, the stores of North Pembroke came and went, not unlike today, each providing some important service for the time and then fading into memory. Each and every one served to help the residents of Pembroke build our town into a thriving community and set down the base on which we continue to build for the future.

WATER STREET AND THE TWO MILE

Next time you take the Water Street "shortcut" between Route 53 and Route 139, slow down and take the time to observe the scenery in an area that played an interesting part in pre-Pembroke history.

In 1636, seventy-six years before the incorporation of the town of Pembroke, the people of Scituate were concerned that they did not have enough land for their subsistence. What they needed was more meadowland on which to farm because so much of Scituate was salt marsh.

In 1640, the general court decided that they should have set off for them on the east side of the North River a section of land "two miles in length and a mile in breadth, if it be there to be had." This grant of land, which had been mostly part of Duxbury, became known as the "Two Mile" and today encompasses most of Water Street (originally known as Two Mile Road) from Robinson's Creek to the North River. The entire grant was finally established in 1658.

Duxbury, which was becoming increasingly alarmed by continual annexation of land by Scituate, deeded to the minister of the First Parish Church of Duxbury, Reverend John Holmes, one hundred acres of land that was bounded by Robinson's Creek. In 1665, the general court confirmed Scituate's right to the Two Mile and declared that Robinson's Creek was the boundary between Scituate and Duxbury. This meant that this newly acquired piece of Scituate and its inhabitants were completely shut off from the rest of Scituate by the North River.

The residents of the Two Mile area began to complain that they were receiving no benefit from either the Scituate school or the church for which they were being taxed. After 1712, they began to request to be transferred to the new town of Pembroke. In June 1728, their petition, accompanied by a similar one from the Town of Pembroke, was presented in the general court by Samuel Hatch and six other residents of the Two Mile. Copies of the petitions were ordered to be sent to Scituate, which was to answer to the general court at its fall session.

The petitions failed, and it was another ten years before similar petitions were again presented to the general court by Pembroke and Two Mile residents John Magoun, John Magoun Jr., Isaac Hatch and Job Randall. This time, they were successful, and this part of the Two Mile became part of Pembroke.

Today, Water Street is dead-ended by Route 3. On the other side of the highway is the town of Marshfield and an area known as "Two Mile Farm" that was actually the northern end of the Two Mile grant. Water Street is dotted with lovely old homes, some dating back to the time of the Two Mile dispute. Former Pembroke Historical Commission member Donald Shute noted that this section of Pembroke's Two Mile is somewhat unusual in that it contains five separate family burial grounds.

Part VII

UNIQUELY PEMBROKE

The Pembroke Bee

A number of years ago, *Yankee* magazine came to town to cover our annual fish fry held each May at Tommy Reading Park—aka the Herring Run. As they traveled around our town, the *Yankee* crew also discovered our former Center Library (now the senior center) cupola adorned with its unique bee.

When I first moved into town and noticed the bee (it isn't always something you notice right away), my family speculated that it might have something to do with the abundance of cranberry bogs and the importance of bees to their cultivation every year. I was delighted to learn, after some investigation, that the bee had a more historical significance—it was a symbol of the annual spelling "bee" held each spring. This custom began in 1875 when funds were needed to stock a free library in Pembroke, and a public spelling bee was held for that purpose.

Pembroke's first free public library was the result of the combining of the assets of two social reading clubs in town, the Female Reading Society, which was founded in 1811 but had ceased to exist, and the Pembroke Reading Club on May 4, 1875. It was decided then that a prize spelling school (bee) and miscellaneous entertainment should be held, the proceeds of which would benefit a circulating library. The Pembroke Free Library was established in 1878.

The bee on the library cupola, designed by noted Pembroke artist Richard Edlund, was unveiled at the 100th anniversary of the Pembroke Library in

The Pembroke bee atop the old public library, now the Council on Aging building. *Pembroke Historical Society.*

May 1975. It became the symbol for the library at the suggestion of former chairman of the board of library trustees Alan Dunphy. In *Pembroke Revisited*, the 1976 publication of the Pembroke Bicentennial Committee, Mr. Edlund described the bee's construction as follows:

> *Height, 47 inches; width (widest of stance), 46 inches; length (of body), 35 inches; weight, 45 pounds. Construction is similar to that of a ship, consisting of flat ribs and braces of quarter-inch plywood over which bronze and copper screening was applied. The legs were formed of one-inch aluminum tubing…The lightweight durable skin is of a thermosetting plastic pressed into the screening. The wings are three-eighths inch marine plywood bolted to aluminum plate.*

All in all, the effect is stunning, and it appears that *Yankee* magazine discovered something that most residents of Pembroke have known all along: Pembroke has a special appeal, even in New England, which prides itself on being unique, full of Yankee ingenuity and cleverness. We exhibit all that and so much more!

THE BRYANTVILLE FOUNTAIN

The history of the town of Pembroke overflows with events and names of citizens who played important roles in the history not only of our area but also of the nation. They are part of our legacy, and many of us never tire of hearing about them.

However, from time to time, it is interesting to learn about the lesser-known stories that, while not particularly earth shaking, are at least reflections of the local color that makes each small New England town unique unto itself and provides us, yet again, with a glimpse of the residents of our town who have gone before us.

One such story was related to us in 1976 during the celebration of the American Bicentennial. Marjorie Smith, a member of the Bicentennial Committee and co-editor of the booklet *Pembroke Revisited*, told of the "mystery of the Bryantville fountain." It was based on the lead story in the November 6, 1907 issue of the *Bryantville News*.

The occasion was the dedication of a bronze drinking fountain that had been erected in Bryantville Square. It was presented to the Town of Pembroke by the members of the South Hanson Woman's Christian Temperance Union. It stood fourteen feet high, and the Brockton Water Department had promised to provide free drinking water forever to fill it.

In her article, Ms. Smith noted that, sixty-eight years later, the fountain was missing. She decided to take up the search. She began by poring over

The old Bryantville fountain. *Pembroke Historical Society.*

page after yellowed page of the *Bryantville News* looking for references to the fountain. From time to time, she found it mentioned, especially in relation to fire chief Horatio Daub, who was praised for keeping the fountain from freezing over the winter so that the horses could continue to drink from it.

Ms. Smith also talked to such older Pembroke residents as Melvin Shepherd Sr., who remembered breaking the white glass globe on top of the fountain's tall shaft one day in about 1910 as he tried to water his thirsty horse. Mr. Shepherd remembered that it cost his father twenty-two dollars to replace the globe.

Ms. Smith finally found the answer to her mystery from Pembroke resident Mrs. Helen Erikson, former Pembroke postmistress who just remembered the fountain when it was being used as a goldfish pool behind Ira Porter's store in Pembroke Center. By that time, the tall shaft and globe were gone. She believed that since automobile transportation had almost completely replaced the old horse and wagon, the fountain had become obsolete.

Mr. Porter entrusted the fountain into Mrs. Erikson's care when he left town. She eventually turned over the fountain base to the Pembroke Grange. Mrs. Doris Anderson and her husband had moved the fountain to the Herring Run. Each spring, Grange members planted it with flowers. At one point, the entire base disappeared from the Herring Run. It was tracked down again by Doris Anderson and was eventually moved to the front lawn of the Pembroke Historical Society, where the tradition of spring flower planting continues to this day.

Bryantville News

On February 18, 1903, the residents of the Bryantville section of Pembroke were presented with a rare and probably unwitting opportunity to record for posterity the daily goings-on in their lives. It was on this date that the first issue of the *Bryantville News* hit the streets of the village.

Publisher George Edward Lewis had moved from Franconia, New Hampshire, to Bryantville as a teenager with his family in 1884 and had brought with him a dream to make the art of the printed word available to all. Along with co-publisher George A. Turner, Mr. Lewis began a publication filled with snippets of the daily lives of the locals—stories of births, marriages, deaths, visits from distant family members, robberies, fires, weather events, church news and just about every social event that took place

Bryantville News

Vol. I - No. I | Bryantville, Mass., February 18, 1903 | Price Two cents

Introduction.

"WHAT'S THE NEWS?" This is usually one of the first remarks when one meets a friend, and we imagine it will be one of the first when your eye meets this the first issue of our little paper.

We hope as you read the succeeding weekly numbers that the question will be answered, but we will try in a few words to tell you what we hope to make it.

The "News" will be published in the interest of this part of the County, and will print local items, and others, of interest to all.

The "News" will be independent in politics, standing for those principles which tend for the good of all concerned, and supporting for office the best men irrespective of party.

We shall be pleased to publish all notices of Church Services, regular and special, and all matters of interest concerning these bodies.

Other societies will find us glad to print accounts of meetings and progress of work in their various branches.

We hope for your kind recognition of our efforts and a spirit to overlook our faults, and with a support which will give us strength to overcome our difficulties one by one.

With all this to encourage us we shall endeavor to keep our paper a clean bright sheet, to print news which you might not get in any other way, to print "the truth and nothing but the truth" as far as in us lies.

Yours for progress,
Geo. Edward Lewis,
Geo. A. Turner,
Publishers.

Take heart of grace and look before,
Instead of backward, on the way;
Wash out the old regretful score,
The sorrowing sins of yesterday.
For what's the world and all its days
But ours to try and try again?
Not ours to falter on its ways,
Not ours to fling aside for pain.
Take heart of grace, then, day by day;
Take heart of grace and sing each morn,
"To-day's to-day, not yesterday,
And all the world is newly born."
—*Nora Perry.*

The boys of the section of Nantasket Beach known as Waveland have formed what they call the Waveland life saving crew, with the object of caring for stray cats, left at the beach by summer residents. This organization will have plenty of time to get into good running order before called into service when the summer colony departs next fall. Guy Ettinger is captain, and the patrolmen include Manuel Antone, Horace Ettinger, Philip Hatchard, George Johnson, Harold Hatchard, Frank Gould and George Thorburne.

BRYANTVILLE

Death of Mrs. Georgiana Luther.

On Wednesday February 11th Mrs. Georgiana Luther passed away after a short illness of pneumonia. Mrs. Luther was born in January, 1846, her parents being Capt. and Mrs. E. E. K. Gurney, and she was one of eleven children, only two of whom remain, Miss Josie and Mr. Thomas Gurney. Mrs. Luther was married in 1866 to Edward Y. Luther, who died in 1875. They had three children, all of them surviving her, Grace G. Luther, Mrs. Dana Pratt and Ada J. Luther. The funeral took place Friday at one o'clock, from her late home on Main St., Rev. D. M. Cleveland officiating. Many beautiful floral offerings expressed the respect and esteem in which the deceased was held by her many friends and their deep sympathy for the bereaved daughters. Among them were: Spray of roses, callas and carnations, daughters; Spray of American beauty roses, Mr. and Mrs. Wendell W. Bryant; spray white roses, Mr. and Mrs. Henry Bryant; spray hyacinths and roses, Mrs. G. Towsend; spray callas, C. Y. Howard and wife; Wreath pupils of Hastings School, Whitman, spray, teachers of Hastings School, of Whitman; spray of pinks, Lulu Wood; spray of pinks; Warren Howard and wife; spray callas and roses, Warren Hill and wife; Hyacinths and roses, Geo. Howland and wife; Roses, Edw. E. Hill and wife; Roses, Luke K. Hemmenway; Wreath, W. R. Corps; Carnations, Chas. Cogan and wife; Roses, Mrs. F. Chamberlain and Mrs. J. Ellis Chamberlain; English violets, Mrs. Sarah Oakes; Roses, Miss Amy DeWitt. The bearers were: Geo. E. Bickford, Edwin Pratt, Nathaniel T. Howland and Nathaniel Morton.

Rev. R. S. Cushman's sermon Sun. morning Feb. 15th, was upon Abraham Lincoln, it being the anniversary of his birth. The thought of the discourse was "Lincoln, God's Instrument." The pulpit was draped with the national colors and resting against it a fine picture of Lincoln, draped with bunting. Special music had been prepared but owing to the prevalence of sore throats had to be omitted.

The L. A. S. will meet at Mrs. C. E. Keene's Thursday afternoon.

The W. C. T. meets at Mrs. J. Reed's.

The Junior Church of Bryantville is a new organization of young people under the supervision of Rev. and Mrs. R. S. Cushman. Merle Benson President, Edith Bourne, Secretary, and Florence Turner, Treasurer.

On Feb. 23rd Mrs. O. W. Charles will read a paper entitled "A Minister and a General in the Revolutionary War," before Deborah Sampson Chapter, D. A. R., of Brockton.

Florence Turner is quite ill with the grip, from which her mother is just recovering.

The Registrars of Voters met at Dr. O. W. Charles' Saturday evening. Seven names were taken from the list. Five of these are deceased.

Snow Storm

Worst of the Season.

Electrics Blockaded

Mails However Went Through by Team

The storm of Monday increased rapidly in the night and Tuesday resembled a blizzard. Altho the local and long distance telephone lines were in fine order the electric road was completely blocked. The snow plow was kept running during the day but the mails were carried to and brought from Whitman by C. E. Crowell.
The first car toward Whitman was at 4:25 P. M. and there was no general service after that.

E. E. Hill is confined to the house by a severe cold; and his clerk, Charles Howe of Centre Pembroke is also ill at home.

Miss Josie Gurney and her companion Miss. Holmes, who has been so ill, have with them Miss. Cummings, who was formerly Miss. Gurney's companion.

It is learned from good authority that the managers of Mayflower Grove will offer the public among other attractions the coming season, a novelty in this vicinity. This being something in the form of a "Chute", and will be popular with the bathers.

The subject for the morning service Sunday Feb. 22nd at the M. E. Church, "The King," John 18-36.

The Sunday School Class of Lawrence Reed has formed a social club, holding their weekly meetings in Benson's Cafe Wed. evenings. Games are played and a pleasant evening spent.
All boys desirious of joining must first become members of the S. S. class.

Friends and neighbors are glad to welcome back Chas. F. Howard and wife, after three months spent in Maine.

Mrs. Helen Josselyn of Centre Pembroke is keeping house for the Misses Grace and Ada Luther.

On Wednesday night Feb. 11th Mr Harrison Bearce died at his home on Main St., Mr. Bearce was one of a large family not many of whom remain. He was 80 years of age and had long been in poor health. The funeral services were Sunday afternoon from his late home, conducted by Rev. D. M. Cleveland
Among the many floral offerings were; spray of pink roses, wife; spray of white roses, W. P. Bearce and family; floral piece, H. L. Bearce and family; spray of hyacinths and narcissus, W. P. Bearce Jr. and Miss. Packard; spray of callas and myrtle, Mr. and Mrs. S. T. Niles, Mrs. Hiram Stevens, George Tew, Mrs. Lewis Bunce; spray of daffodils, Mrs. A. C. Brigham; spray of hyacinths, Mrs. C. E. Allen and Mrs. N. S. Sturtevant; spray of cut flowers, Mrs. D. M. Cleveland, spray of roses, Mr. and Mrs. Wm. Lieber. The bearers were, John Willis, N. T. Howland, Robert Calder, and Gibson Beal.

It gives us pleasure to greet our old customers, and to introduce ourselves, thus, to you whom we desire to call new ones.

We have a Complete Stock of

Drug Store Goods,

Toilet Articles, Trusses

and make a Specialty of

Fine Rubber Goods,

at Right Prices.

Agents for
Eastman's Kodaks, Films, and Developing Machines.

H. C. Cleveland,
Druggist
11 So. Avenue, - Whitman, Mass.

When Papa's Sick.

When papa's sick, my goodness sakes!
Such awful, awful times it makes!
He speaks in oh! such lonesome t
And gives such ghastly kind of gro
And rolls his eyes and holds his
And makes ma help him up to bed;
While Sis and Bridget run to heat
Hot water bags to warm his feet,
And I must get the doctor quick—
We have to jump when papa's sick.

When papa's sick ma has to stand
Right side the bed and hold his hand,
While Sis she has to fan an' fan,
For he says he's "a dyin' man."
And wants the children round him to
Be there when "sufferin' pa gets through;"
He says he wants to say good-bye
And kiss us all and then he'll die;
Then moans and says his "breathin's thick"—
It's awful sad when papa's sick.

When papa's sick he acts that way
Until he hears the doctor say,
"You've only got a cold, you know,
You'll be all right in a day or so."
And then—Well, say, you ought to see,
He's different as he can be,
And growls and swears from noon to night
Just 'cause his dinner ain't cooked right,
And all he does is fuss and kick—
We're all used up when papa's sick.
—*Joe Lincoln in L. A. W. Bulletin.*

It is announced from London that Madam Adeline Patti has finally signed a contract for sixty concerts in America, commencing Nov. 3rd next.

Parker—"What's wrong? You seem worried."

Streeter—"I am. I wrote two notes—one to my brother, asking him if he took me for a fool, and the other to Miss Golding asking her if she would be mine. While I was out somebody telephoned 'Yes,' and I don't know which of 'em it was."—*Chicago News.*

The city of Portland, Me. is to be the important point in next summer's joint army and navy maneuvres.

February 18, 1903 inaugural issue of the *Bryantville News*. *Pembroke Historical Society.*

in the area. If it happened to you and you lived in Bryantville, you could probably read about it in the pages of the *News*. Of course, unlike many of the publications of today, lurid and distasteful details were never even hinted at, and life may have seemed just a bit too perfect, but such was the climate of the time.

Bryantville News print shop. *Pembroke Historical Society.*

Eventually, the *News* began to include poems written by locals as well as short and episodic stories from other parts of the country. It added columns of advice for women, tips for farmers and projects for the "young folks." All this for two cents an issue or a dollar per year—published every Wednesday.

And then there were the advertisements. Every local drugstore, millinery shop, clothier, hardware store, grocer and undertaker wanted to see its ad printed in the *Bryantville News*. There were ads for patent medicines that promised to cure everything from the common cold to sciatica.

The stated purpose of the paper said it all: "We shall endeavor to keep our paper a clean, bright sheet, to print news which you might not get in any other way, to 'print the truth and nothing but the truth' as far as in us lies."

ICING IN PEMBROKE

Today, with air conditioners, refrigeration and automatic ice makers, it may be hard for us to understand the importance of natural ice to earlier generations of Americans, especially in the nineteenth century. The very size

Icing on Oldham Pond. The icehouse was on Mattakeesett Street. *Pembroke Historical Society.*

of the former natural ice industry is staggering. Ice was cut and lifted from ponds, where it was frozen by nature, and was the second highest tonnage item (after cotton) to be shipped or moved by railroads. In Boston, the heart of the natural ice industry, it was not unusual for two hundred freight cars at once, filled with ice, to be waiting at the railroad yards. The banks of many ponds in eastern Massachusetts were lined with ice storage houses. These buildings were of huge proportions, containing many floors and with walls often two feet thick insulated with sawdust. Ships sailed from Boston to ports in the West Indies; London; Calcutta; Charleston, South Carolina; and New Orleans loaded to capacity with ice. Shrinkage from pond to final port was kept to about 50 percent, thanks to fast handling and careful insulation.

Prior to this time, perishable food was sold fresh or stored only in limited quantities and for limited times in the lower areas of deeply dug wells. Local farmhouses had their own small icehouses or cellars, filled with a few tons of ice cut from local ponds.

It was Massachusetts merchant Frederick Tudor who realized that it was possible to ship ice as a profitable commodity to areas where ice was not made naturally. He was a bold trader who negotiated exclusive franchises that helped make his ice ventures profitable.

Pembroke, being graced with numerous ponds, undoubtedly was seldom at a loss for this valuable commodity. While ice was taken from most of the area's ponds, icing on Furnace Pond was done on a larger scale.

Over the century when ice production was big business, the tools and methods of the trade varied somewhat, and there were some regional differences. The basic steps, however, were fairly simple. The first step was to clear the snow, slush and poor-grade ice using horse-drawn scrapers and scoops. Then the thickness of the ice was established—a thickness of fourteen to fifteen inches was standard. The area was then laid out or marked in a grid using a plank and a horse-drawn cutting edge to a depth of about two inches. Then the ice was deep cut, and the edges were caulked with ice chips and slush to keep water from seeping up and freezing the cakes of ice together again. The cakes of ice were separated and floated to the icehouse, where they were lifted using a steam-driven device. The ice was then stored in the icehouse until needed.

The name Jones River Pond was changed to Silver Lake partly because it was believed to be a more pleasing name for an ice company located on the Kingston side of this body of water that is shared by Pembroke, Kingston and Halifax.

The gradual introduction of mechanical ice production and on-the-spot refrigeration caused the end of the ice harvesting industry.

ONCE A SCHOOL, ALWAYS A...RESTAURANT?

Over the years, many of Pembroke's oldest historical buildings have been recycled for other purposes. A former home becomes a bank, a school becomes a community center—there seems to be no end to the creative uses for these architectural gems.

Two structures on Route 53 (Washington Street) have come back over and over as new businesses. Because Washington Street was known historically as the King's Highway (one of several ancient routes from Boston to Plymouth), many of the buildings located along its route have some local historical significance.

These buildings (located to the right of the Pudding Brook Pantry) began as two separate structures. The right side of the building was the North

Pembroke District #8 School. It was a typical one-room schoolhouse, similar to the building that now houses the Pembroke Historical Society Museum at Pembroke Center. It was built in 1848 to replace an earlier structure that had been built in the mid-1700s and was originally located next to the Briggs-Barker Burial Ground on Washington Street. The reason for moving the first schoolhouse is somewhat unusual. The story goes that sometime during the mid-1800s, schoolchildren playing outside at recess accidentally unearthed the body of one of the town's early settlers. The townspeople voted to move the school a quarter of a mile south to the site of the present 1848 building. This second structure was used by the town as a schoolhouse until 1924, when it was sold and used as a private residence.

The left side of the present structure is believed to have been a barn built by Sylvanus Smith in 1840. Mr. Smith was the son of Captain Jonathan Smith of Duxbury. After his marriage, Sylvanus bought the "old Morse place" in Pembroke, where he lived during the years of his partnership with Luther Briggs and Melzar S. Turner. Together, they built ships at the Brick Kiln Ship Yard on the North River in Pembroke. Eventually, Sylvanus Smith moved to East Boston and began the shipbuilding firm of Smith and Townsend with his partner James L. Townsend.

North Pembroke District #8 School with Sylvanus Smith's barn in the background. *Pembroke Historical Society.*

These two buildings were bought by George Turner and, in 1980, were joined together by a sixty-foot addition. Mr. Turner opened a restaurant there called Turner's Prime Tavern. This spot has been the site of several other types of restaurants in recent years.

PEMBROKE'S VERY OWN MOON TREE

If you were living in Pembroke in 1976, you may remember the bicentennial moon tree. If you're a gardener, you're probably wondering what species of tree this might be.

Moon tree

This tiny plant is Pembroke's "moon tree," which was grown from seeds taken to the moon and back on Apollo. Last week the tree was planted in a ceremony at the Adah Hall Pembroke Militia; members of the Pembroke Historical Society and the Bicentennial Committee; Melvin B. Shepherd Sr. and Richard Willis, who were instrumental in getting the tree for Pembroke; Selectmen Chairman Robert Craford; State Rep. Robert Gillette and Tree Warden Robert Reardon. Pembroke is one of only two communities in the state to receive a "moon tree" from the U.S. Forest Service as part of this Bicentennial project.

Pembroke's moon tree seedling. *Pembroke Historical Society.*

Many of us remember the grand celebration that was the nation's 200th birthday—the year of the bicentennial. Products were called "official bicentennial products," and my son, like many other babies who were born in 1976, was officially listed by the hospital as a "bicentennial baby." It was an interesting time of patriotism and pride.

Pembroke's bicentennial coordinator, Richard F. Willis, announced that Pembroke was one of two communities in Massachusetts (the other town was Holliston) selected to receive a "moon tree" as part of a unique project of the United States Forest Service for the bicentennial.

"Moon tree" seedlings were grown from seeds that had traveled to the moon and back in 1971 on Apollo 14. The flight was launched by NASA on January 31, 1971, and returned to earth on February 9. The seeds of sycamore, loblolly pine and sequoia trees were carried in a small container by command module pilot Stuart Roosa because of his strong belief in forest resources. The Forest Service's Institute of Forest Genetics in Gulfport, Mississippi, and the Forest Service Laboratory in Placerville, California, were charged with nurturing the seeds. The seedlings Pembroke received were Sycamore *Platanus occidentalis*, grown at the Mississippi site, and could grow to one hundred feet high and up to ten feet across.

On Sunday, June 6, 1976, the Pembroke Bicentennial Committee and the Pembroke Historical Society held a tree planting like no other. Pembroke militiamen fired a three-volley salute as the tree was planted on the grounds of the Adah Hall House, a historical society property on Barker Street.

Melvin Shepherd Sr., a longtime Pembroke conservation and forestry advocate, was given the honor of planting the tree. Following the ceremony, the Camp Fire Girls Adventure Club provided refreshments.

SCHOOSETT PHONE COMPANY

Verizon, AT&T and T-Mobile are all familiar terms for something we take for granted today: telephone service. No one can or wants to imagine what life in the twenty-first century would be like without this means of communication. I suppose the upside would be no telemarketers, no dinnertime interruptions and no wrong numbers. But on the other hand, there would be no long-distance holiday conversations, no home Internet service and lots of wasted time making needless trips when you could have called. And where would today's businesses be without Internet hookups, faxes and conference calling?

We all remember that until the breakup of AT&T, Ma Bell ruled the phone lines, and smaller phone companies were virtually unheard of or a poor substitute with limited service and poor quality.

If you lived in Pembroke during the first half of the twentieth century, you might have been part of a small but very real thorn in the side of the Bell Telephone System—the Schoosett Telephone Company. This tiny local system came into existence right around the turn of the century and lasted, as far as anyone can determine, until the beginning of World War I.

It is said that the telephones themselves were very well made, all put together carefully by hand. Any parts that might corrode, tarnish or rust were heavily nickel plated. At one time, there were as many as twenty-three of these telephones, all operated from a single wire, with a second wire (for grounding) stuck, quite literally, directly into the ground. The system ran from Simmons Store on Washington Street; up Water Street, where it crossed Schoosett Street; on up to where today's Route 3 blocks the road; and down to the old Hanover bridge—a distance of about five miles all run off a single wire.

The subscribers to the phone system were the only stockholders; there were no officers, no bills to pay—except for maintenance—and no central office. Except for crossing two streets and the North River, the line ran through pastures and woodlots belonging to the subscribers. Your phone number was easy to remember—it was a number between one and twenty-three. You were required to count the number of rings to determine if the call was for you. If your number was twenty-one, then you picked up when the phone stopped ringing after twenty-one times.

An item in a Boston newspaper from shortly before 1914 headed "Schoosett Phone Company Still Functioning…Little Pembroke Outfit Defies Entire World and Scorns Absorption" says it all. The Bell System tried hard to take over the little system only to be told that it was "built by private individuals for private use over private land."

The Bell System tried every method it could think of to legally end the little company but to no avail. Eventually, it gave up, but the little company soon died on its own, leaving behind twenty-three early twentieth-century collector's items to gather dust in attics all over North Pembroke.

PEMBROKE'S TROLLEY

Until the end of the twentieth century, when the new commuter rail line was built, the only form of public transportation in our area had been the Plymouth and Brockton bus lines, but prior to the buses, the way to get around using public transportation was to take the trolley.

Trolley cars came to Pembroke as part of the Brockton and Plymouth Street Railway in 1900. This line merged with the Plymouth and Kingston Street Railway, which had been in existence since 1889, to connect the two large population centers of Plymouth and Brockton. Pembroke's section of this important route ran down School Street (Route 27) from Bryantville to Kingston.

The trolley system was very important to the economic development of the area. Especially in the years prior to the invention of the automobile, it meant that those who could not afford to own or did not have room to keep a horse and buggy could nevertheless travel greater distances to go to work or to shop in stores.

While operating on a year-round basis, ridership was the heaviest on the Brockton and Plymouth Street Railway during the summer months. The entire twenty-six-mile trip from Main Street in Brockton to Plymouth Center took a little more than two hours one way.

One of the greatest traffic stimulants to the Brockton and Plymouth Street Railway's business was Mayflower Grove, which opened for business in May

Brockton and Plymouth trolley. *Pembroke Historical Society.*

1901 and was located on the shore of Little Sandy Pond in Bryantville. The amusement park, built by the owners of the railway to break up the lengthy ride from Plymouth to Brockton, contained a merry-go-round, restaurant, casino, outdoor theater, dancing pavilion and picnic ground. There were also facilities for boating and swimming, and for many years, band concerts were performed on weekends and holidays.

In 1922, the Brockton and Plymouth Street Railway was sold and was reorganized to form the Plymouth and Brockton Street Railway.

As the private automobile became more and more popular and affordable, public transportation was seen as a less convenient mode of travel for the day-to-day needs of the average American. Improvements in local roads and highway construction meant the tearing up of much of the trolley and commuter train tracks, and those sections that remained fell into a state of disrepair. By 1928, buses had taken over the line.

It appears that with the construction of our new commuter rail system, South Shore public transit came full circle, and transportation history indeed repeated itself.

Part VIII

COMMON TASKS

Who's Calling?

Chances are, like so many Americans around the Christmas season, those of us here in Pembroke will take or make the time to visit, either formally or informally, with family, friends or other associates to share holiday cheer. The invitations that often come in the mail reminded me of an article I read recently in a magazine dedicated to antiques. I came across an article about calling cards—the genteel version of today's business card that was used by polite society rather than by hurried businessmen.

In today's fast-paced world, one only needs to think about the explosion of e-mail and text messaging to realize that we rarely have time to visit with friends and neighbors at all—much less leave behind a printed token of a missed opportunity to sit and chat.

In 1869, the author of *The Perfect Gentleman or Etiquette and Elegance* wrote: "[Calling] cards are indispensable to the intercourse of polite society." As late as the 1950s, Emily Post wrote that it was a good idea to have a card tray near the front door.

The idea of visiting cards may have originated in China as far back as the fourteenth century, although it is possible that Roman callers wrote their names with a stylus in a wax tablet kept near the entryway. No such examples are still in existence, but early literature refers to these practices.

During the seventeenth and eighteenth centuries, playing cards had plain white backs, and people frequently used them as calling cards by inscribing

A calling card press. *Photo by John Proctor.*

their names on them. Early Americans also followed this practice, even though card playing was frowned upon, and law forbade the importation of playing cards from Europe.

Eventually, the styles of calling cards progressed from playing card backs to elaborately hand-decorated works of art, crafted by ladies with time on their hands. Simple, embossed cards or highly decorated versions were soon mass-produced in sheets. While the card was decorated, there was a blank area for a person to sign his or her name—preprinted names were often seen as being in poor taste.

So, next time you receive an invitation, either formal or informal, in the mail, tuck it away somewhere for future generations to marvel at—I think e-mail, as wonderful as it is, will someday render these pieces of Pembroke's past obsolete.

CHILD'S PLAY

Traditionally, the month of September reminds us of back-to-school activities and a general gearing up of our own busy lives after the relative calm of the summer. Vacations, for the most part, are but a fading memory, and another year of work, punctuated by occasional moments of "play," stares us in the face.

Today, we tend to think of school as the work of our young people. Many of us adults think back on our childhood fondly as a time when our biggest problems revolved around coming up with ideas for the science fair and whether we'd have enough time to get in an afternoon ballgame or bike ride and still get all our homework done.

I recently read an article about children in nineteenth-century rural New England by Jack Larkin from the *Old Sturbridge Visitor* and rediscovered for myself the fact that perhaps the "good old days" weren't quite so good. Sure, most of our children are required to do chores around the house in addition to their schoolwork, but the life of a child in the 1800s revolved around mostly work and very little play. Children working was a necessary part of our rural economy, and devoid of labor-saving devices, the more children you had, the easier your life was, relatively speaking. Children began their household tasks almost as soon as they could understand the difference between a crop plant and a weed. As they grew older, their jobs became increasingly more difficult. Young girls worked with their mothers learning the daily chores required to maintain family life—cooking, sewing, cleaning, laundry and tending to the dairy, or at least the family cow and the chicken coop. Their brothers were working along with their fathers around the barn and in the fields.

If you happened to be from a poorer family, you might be "hired out" to work for the neighbors doing housework, caring for younger children or hauling firewood for a few cents a day.

Although education was valued by most, its importance often paled in comparison to the need for helping hands around the farm.

While the daily work experiences of children from the nineteenth century are greatly different from those of twenty-first-century children, remarkably, the play of both centuries is somewhat similar. Fantasy games, while vastly different, were played by children of both centuries. Hiking, swimming, skating, jump rope and various team games of ball were enjoyed by children from one hundred years ago as they are today. Perhaps, if you came from a more well-to-do family, you were afforded the luxury of a favorite book or toy.

An unidentified young member of Pembroke's Keene family with his favorite book and toy. *Pembroke Historical Society.*

This article pointed out something I found interesting: children today spend most of their non-school hours playing, while play was an afterthought for children of early New England. Perhaps the children of Pembroke's past enjoyed their playtime much more for that reason.

WOMEN'S WORK, TWENTIETH-CENTURY STYLE

I love old-fashioned household hints. If you have ever read my columns in the past, you'll find hints for gardening, self-medication and all types of other subjects gleaned from all sorts of places. One of my favorite sources is the *Bryantville News*, which began publication in 1903 and ceased about 1906. These tips offer a glimpse into the everyday concerns of our forebears. This particular local publication frequently offered sections called "Woman's World," "For the Housewife," "Women's Interests"—well, you get the idea. These articles give us a peek at our grandmother's concerns (at least as seen by the men who published the paper) and a look at the ideas of the Heloises of an earlier time.

Let's take a look at a section called, appropriately enough, "Laundry Lines":

> *Frequent rubbing on sandpaper will keep irons from sticking.*
>
> *Laundry tubs will not warp or crack if the precaution is taken to put a pail of water into each directly after use.*
>
> *A lump of alum the size of a hickory nut added to each pint of starch will keep the colors of calicoes and ginghams bright a long time.*
>
> *Don't wash dainty, perishable needlework with ordinary soap. Make suds of the white sort and when washed iron wet upon the wrong side.*
>
> *Before using the rope you have bought for a new clothesline, boil it and let it dry. In this way it is properly shrunk and it is also made more durable.*
>
> *A little pipe clay dissolved in the water used in washing linen saves a great deal of labor and soap and cleans the dirtiest linen thoroughly. This method is especially useful in towns where outdoor bleaching is generally an impossibility.*
>
> *Half a lemon placed in the water in which dish towels and kitchen cloths are soaked is said to sweeten them wonderfully.*
>
> *If a bowl or deep plate of quicklime is kept in a damp closet it will prevent clothes that are hung there from becoming mildewed. The lime should be renewed when it becomes slack.*

I found it interesting that so much space was taken up with the pursuit of impeccable laundry. Various fabrics and, of course, whites were treated differently, but since today most of our colored cottons far outnumber our "whites," I have included directions for laundering here. For the best way to launder colored cotton fabrics and keep colors bright:

> *Have ready starch and a large tubful of rinsing water. Have a half tubful of very soapy lukewarm water and leave the soap in the water while washing. Turn the garments wrong side out and wash, rinse, starch and hang in the shade, finishing one piece before wetting the next. Do not rub soap into the material unless it is very much soiled. Let the clothes lie, sprinkled for a very short time and iron on the wrong side with irons barely hot enough to dry the goods nicely. Turn and press hems and seams on the right side. In this way the little girl's school dresses can be bright and fresh all summer.*

Imagine going through those steps for *each* of our colored garments. No wonder our foremothers allowed a full day for laundry—often Monday.

And lastly, my personal favorite:

> *For all your clothing worn in the daytime, footwear included—open out and hang over chairs or on hooks near the stove or heat register to dry*

> *and air during the night. If you neglect this simple sanitary measure, your clothing will feel damp and cold in the morning because it still contains the evaporations from your body during the previous day and after a while your clothing will have an unpleasant odor from these evaporations. Drying and airing your footwear during the night will keep your feet from sweating, coldness and bad odors.*

My washer and dryer have never looked more appealing!

With regard to spring cleaning, let's face it, every year, when the months of March and April roll around, it means it's time to start to think about spring cleaning—that less than glorious spring ritual that gets rid of the stale, closed-up air that languished in the house all winter. This requires, among other things, that I dust and wash every nook and cranny and, oh yeah, get the cat fur off the upholstery.

The proper way to clean things around the house was another frequent topic—no all-purpose cleaners for these women. Each item had a special homemade concoction and technique. For example, when cleaning windows, "An easy way to clean windows is to make a paste of mild soapsuds and whiting and let it dry on the windows. Then wipe it off and polish with an old cotton cloth. Old cotton is the best to use, as it will leave no lint. If the glass is very soiled, it is best to wash it with soapsuds and ammonia before using the paste."

No wonder "a woman's work was never done."

BIBLIOGRAPHY

Lewis, George Edward. *Old Pembroke*. Bryantville, MA: George Edward Lewis, 1912.

Litchfield, Henry Wheatland. *Ancient Landmarks of Pembroke*. Bryantville, MA: George Edward Lewis, 1910.

New England Historic Genealogical Society. AmericanAncestors.org.

———. *Vital Records of Pembroke, MA to 1850*. Boston: F.H. Gilson Company, 1911.

Pembroke Bicentennial Committee. *Pembroke Revisited*. Pembroke, MA: Pembroke Bicentennial Committee, 1962.

Pembroke Historical Commission. *Inventory of Historic Properties*. Pembroke, MA: Pembroke Historical Commission, n.d.

Pembroke Historical Society. Old house files, family files and miscellaneous files.

Pembroke 250th Anniversary Committee. *Town of Pembroke 250th Anniversary 1712 to 1962*. North Abington, MA: Sanderson Brothers, 1962.

Pembroke 275th Anniversary Committee. *Pembroke—Evolution of a New England Township, 1712–1987*. Pembroke, MA: Claremont Press, 1987.

Quill, Ed. *Pembroke 2000*. Pembroke, MA: Ric Sivigny, Desktop Publishing, 2000.

Secretary of the Commonwealth of Massachusetts. *Massachusetts Soldiers and Sailors of the Revolutionary War*. Boston: Wright and Foster Printing Company, 1906

Smith, Susan A. *A Memorial of Rev. Thomas Smith*. Plymouth, MA: Avery and Doten Book and Job Printers, 1895.

ABOUT THE AUTHOR

Karen Cross Proctor has lived with her family in Pembroke for over thirty years. She is the eighth-great-granddaughter of Robert Barker, Pembroke's first settler. She has been the research director of the Pembroke Historical Society for twenty-eight years and is a former member of the Pembroke Historical Commission. For twenty years, she wrote local history columns for the *Pembroke Mariner* and later for the *Pembroke Express*. She is the author of *Pembroke*, an Images of America publication, and *In the Beginning: The First 300 Years of the First Church in Pembroke* and co-author of *Pembroke: Ancient Trails to the Twenty-first Century*.